WOMEN OF FAITH™
STUDY GUIDE SERIES

LIVING A LIFE
OF BALANCE

FOREWORD BY

MARILYN
MEBERG

THOMAS NELSON
Since 1798

NASHVILLE   DALLAS   MEXICO CITY   RIO DE JANEIRO   BEIJING

Published by Thomas Nelson, Inc.
P.O. Box 141000, Nashville, Tennessee, 37214.

Thomas Nelson, Inc. titles may be purchased in bulk for educational, business,
fund-raising, or sales promotional use. For information, please e-mail
SpecialMarkets@ThomasNelson.com.

ISBN-10: 0-7852-5263-0
ISBN-13: 978-0-7852-5263-4

13 14 15 QG 3 0 2 9 2 8

✦ CONTENTS ✦

✦ FOREWORD ✦

I went through a phase of motherhood, which to me, seemed wise, nurturing, and imperative. My husband, Ken, called that period "Marilyn's stone-ground, sugarless" phase. I was convinced the only way to ensure the health and well-being of my family was to avoid as much processed food as possible. Therefore, I made my own bread from stone ground whole wheat flour available to me from Knott's Berry Farm where the old grist mill was still in daily operation. I made my own yogurt, was fanatical about fresh fruit and vegetables, and of course, sugar was an unknown staple in my kitchen.

Now I must admit with blackstrap molasses as the only sweetener I'd consider using, my food could be described as "bracing." But I felt enormously gratified that I was seeing to the nutritional well-being of my family even though there was limited encouragement of my efforts.

One morning, Mary, one of my neighbors, dropped by for a cup of tea (straight, no sugar). I was stunned when she told me that my children were going from house to house asking if there were any available cookies they might snack on. Everyone in that little cul-de-sac knew my food philosophy and felt sorry for my children. Apparently there was an unending supply available for their little sugar-deprived bodies. Mary told me Jeff was especially partial to Mystic Mint Cookies, so she made sure she always had some in her pantry.

In those days no one had heard of staging an "intervention" for those who would benefit from such a truth-filled encounter, but in essence, that was Mary's purpose in dropping by for tea. I needed a touch of truth. At first I felt slightly betrayed by my neighbors, but as I thought more about it, I wondered if my food philosophy was a little out of balance with the world around me. It was certainly out of balance with my neighbors.

As I was discussing it all with Ken that evening (the intervention day), he said that there were times when he wondered if a loaf of nutrition-laden bread might not make a better "door stop" than breakfast food. I began to giggle over that image. I asked him why he had never said anything to me. He said, "Because your heart was so right and your intentions were so pure that I didn't want to say anything. Besides, I figured the kids would mutiny sooner or later anyway and then we could talk."

We had a little family counsel meeting that night and discussed that I was committed to my nutrition program, but I assured everyone I could compromise some. I agreed to Mystic Mints in the pantry (no more than two a day) and we had a little funeral service for the remaining blackstrap molasses. I continued to make my stone ground whole wheat bread, eliminating not only the molasses but the Brewers Yeast as well, which lightened it up and made it much tastier. My family congratulated me.

Ken grew up in a Norwegian-dominated section of Seattle. Mrs. Walvick, who lived next door to his family, was a colorful little lady with predictable patterns and inflexible food habits. Every Saturday morning, she went to her special Norwegian bakery where she would buy bread, rolls, and cold cuts for Saturday night sandwiches. Every Saturday morning, she'd lean into the butcher's ear for the usual instruction regarding the slicing of her cold cuts. "Not too tick and not too tin," she'd whisper and step back, confident the butcher knew exactly what she expected from his slicer.

On the night of our family chat that challenged me to lighten up on my nutritional program, I told Ken that Mrs. Walvick served as an inspiration for me. The "not too tick and not too tin" instruction to the butcher could serve me well. Mrs. Walvick wanted balance for her cold cuts. That was achieved by not going too far in either direction. A touch of Norwegian wisdom warmly inspired me to check my own "tick or tin." Now before we close the subject of my health food inclinations, I will simply say that I still prefer stone ground whole wheat bread, fresh fruits, and vegetables, but a little chocolate has a way of making it all worthwhile, especially a Mystic Mint Cookie with my afternoon tea.

When we consider the life of Jesus and the example He left us, would you say He was careful about "not too tick and not too tin"? Do you think He was balanced? You will remember He sometimes moved away from the clamoring needs of the crowd so that He might be alone; that meant many needs went unmet. He also ate with disreputable people and spent time with persons rejected by their own society. Did Jesus go too far in preferring the company of sinners? Did He spend too much time alone and in prayer?

In this study guide, *Living a Life of Balance*, you will have the fascinating opportunity to examine your own "tick or tin" way of being. How do you see your level of balance? How does it measure up to the example we have of Jesus' life and the Bible's encouragement for each of us to live lives of balance? Sometimes we need to be encouraged by others to see ourselves as we really are. (I most definitely needed that from my neighbor, Mary.)

In whichever way you choose to evaluate yourself as you begin your "balance" study, do know that it is wonderfully possible to give a little, add a little, and rest a little. God means for you to live in equilibrium and balance. How do I know? I've been working on it for years. God meets me where I am even if I'm occasionally a bit more "tick" than "tin."

—*Marilyn Meberg*

✦ INTRODUCTION ✦

Mobiles. Whether constructed from pipe cleaners and yarn, or copper tubing and glass balls, they're pieces of art. A mobile is a pretty affair, strung together with care, its parts in tenuous equilibrium, and hung where it can be gently moved by passing air currents. It suspends from a single point, but gradually fans out to include a complex array of items, each poised upon its own thread. The secret to a good mobile is balance. Each piece is placed in careful conjunction to the others, so that they offset each other. They hang in a pretty symmetry, delicately balanced. If you were to take away just one bauble from this painstaking arrangement, the whole mobile would hang askew. Balance would be lost. And if you tried to add something new to the array, it would wobble off kilter. Balance would be lost again.

So many of us yearn for balance in our lives. We hope to find that precise alignment which will leave all our daily responsibilities in perfect harmony. But as believers, we seem to have so many more ways to be thrown off-balance. We aren't just balancing our household schedules with work, diet, rest, and exercise. No ma'am! That might take care of physical balance. But we must also consider the spiritual balance of our lives. What is the state of our heart? How are we handling the tenuous balance between faith and sight, between love and obedience, between longing and contentment?

This study doesn't come with a pocket organizer and promotional video—*12 Lessons to a Better, More Balanced You!* But it starts at the heart of things. We can hardly expect our physical routine to give us the balanced lifestyle we long for if our hearts are out of kilter. Why not start within, and allow the Lord to work through the intricacies until we can find the equilibrium we need?

"This is how you raise your standard of living!
A safe and stable way to live.
A nourishing, satisfying way to live."

Isaiah 33:16 MSG

CHAPTER 1

THE JUGGLING ACT

"THERE IS A NATURAL BODY, AND THERE IS A SPIRITUAL BODY."

1 Corinthians 15:44 NKJV

No circus would be complete without a juggling act. We watch in amazement as a team of men and women in sequined attire enter the ring. They nod and bow to the audience as they're introduced, then quickly fall into their routine. At first, it seems simple enough. Three balls, then four, then five, then six, then seven. Some begin lofting clubs, hoops, and fragile plates. Then the pattern of flying paraphernalia becomes more complicated, with crisscrossing flight paths. Then, an element of danger is added as long-blade knives and flaming torches are flung through the air. We hold our breaths, gasp in suspense, and applaud with appreciation throughout the jugglers'

CLEARING
✦ THE ✦
COBWEBS

If you could run away and join the circus, what part would you want to take in the show?

demonstration. And all the while, we wonder how they manage to make it look so easy. Even during the most complex display, each of the jugglers smiles broadly. They never miss a pass or drop a ball. Their juggling act appears completely effortless.

Our lives seem like juggling acts. We don't toss balls and clubs in the air, but we're wearing many hats and managing various responsibilities and juggling several schedules. Work schedules, school schedules, practice schedules, exercise schedules. Meal plans, reading plans, budget plans, and vacation plans. Grocery lists, to-do lists, laundry lists, and wish lists. Some people we know manage to find the proper balance in their daily routines, and they keep a smile on their face. *How* do they manage to make it look so easy? We know from experience—it's no easy trick to keep it all airborne, and to our great despair, we keep dropping the ball.

Have you ever been so frustrated that you exclaimed, "I could just lie down right here and die"? I have. Of course I didn't mean it. That was just the most startling thing I could say at the moment, and I wanted somebody to understand I was unraveling. I've always been a bit of a drama queen.

Patsy Clairmont

1. In an effort to keep balance in our lives, we feel like we're in a juggling act. On the one hand, we have life's physical needs to consider. Bills—grocery bills, doctor's bills, utility bills, repair bills, school bills. But what does Jesus remind us of in Luke 12:22, 23?

2. We hear so much about a balanced life these days. We're urged to get more sleep and more exercise. We're supposed to have balanced diets and balanced checkbooks. But as believers, we also have to consider the balance between our physical needs and our spiritual needs. What comparison does Paul draw in 1 Timothy 4:8?

3. In order for anything to balance, it must have a sturdy foundation. We cannot expect to live a balanced life if we do not have a sound base. Both Solomon and Paul spoke much of having something sound at the heart. Match up these examples.

___ Proverbs 2:7   a. God gives a spirit of power and a sound mind.

___ Proverbs 3:21   b. We may be sound in the faith.

___ Proverbs 8:14   c. Keep sound wisdom and discretion.

___ 2 Timothy 1:7   d. By sound doctrine we may convict and exhort.

___ 2 Timothy 1:13   e. Hold fast the pattern of sound words.

___ 2 Timothy 4:3   f. God stores up sound wisdom for the upright.

___ Titus 1:9   g. Counsel is mine, and sound wisdom.

___ Titus 1:13   h. Many will not endure sound doctrine.

*S*triking the proper balance may require us to simplify our lives, for the more responsibilities we have, the more difficult it is to keep all the balls aloft. Paring back on earthly cares allows us to focus on spiritual ones. That's why nuns of old took vows of poverty and chastity. Without all their time taken up by caring for house and husband and children, they could live to minister to the needs of others. We also have more time for our Christian brothers and sisters if we aren't overworked, overextended, and overwhelmed. Could simplification help put your life into better balance?

4. In the Parable of the Sower, Jesus tells His disciples about the conditions needed for His Word to take root, flourish, and bear fruit. What stood in the way of one heart's fruitfulness, according to Luke 8:14?

5. Consider for a moment—why do we want to have balanced lives? Is it so that we can live comfortably, happily, undisturbed? Or is it so that we can give proper time and attention to God's purposes for us? We are here to bear fruit!

John 15:2 — "Every _____ in Me that does not _____ _____ He takes away; and every _____ that _____ _____ He _____, that it may bear _____ _____ " (NKJV).

John 15:16 — "You did not _____ Me, but I _____ you and _____ you that you should _____ and _____ _____, and that your _____ should _____ " (NKJV).

6. A balanced life pays heed to both the physical and spiritual needs of our bodies. A balanced life thrives and bears fruit.

• What does John 15:4 say we must do in order to bear fruit?

• What does John 15:8 say is the result of a fruitful life?

If my mind becomes cluttered by the day's annoyances, it's a given that sooner or later I'm going to lose my self-control. If I lose my self-control, for sure I'm going to lose my joy. I hate losing my joy. Fortunately, I have a choice in how I react.

Marilyn Meberg

DIGGING DEEPER

The balance we seek in the juggling of our many daily requirements must begin in our hearts. Both our physical and spiritual needs must be taken into account. Here are a handful of verses which will help you dig a little deeper into our studies for this week.

- Romans 6:12
- Romans 8:13
- 1 Corinthians 6:20
- 1 Corinthians 9:27
- Philippians 1:20

PONDER & PRAY

Spend a little time this week considering what your physical needs are and what your spiritual needs are. How do they affect one another? What happens when either one is given the greater balance of your time and attention? Also, make it your prayer that the Lord will show you how to abide in Him. We weren't meant to live balanced lives just for our own peace of mind, but so that we can be fruitful. What do you suppose that might mean in your own life?

TRINKETS TO TREASURE

At the close of every Women of Faith conference, women are asked to play a little game of pretend. Each conference guest is asked to imagine that a gift has been placed in her hands—one from each of the speakers—to serve as reminders of the different lessons shared. This study guide will carry on this tradition! At the close of each lesson, you will be presented with a small gift. Though imaginary, it will serve to remind you of the things you have learned. Think of it as a souvenir. Souvenirs are little trinkets we pick up on our journeys to remind us of where we have been. They keep us from forgetting the path we have traveled. Hide these little treasures in your heart, for as you ponder them, they will draw you closer to God.

TRINKET TO TREASURE

We're often so busy trying to maintain balance for all of our physical needs that we hardly have a moment to think of our spiritual ones. This week's trinket is a set of juggling balls. When we look around at others who seem to make balanced living so effortless, we needn't despair when we've dropped the ball. Physical balance, like juggling, takes practice and effort. But even more important is our spiritual balance, which requires a sound heart, a dependence on Jesus, and fruitful lives.

✦ NOTES & PRAYER REQUESTS ✦

CHAPTER 2

BALANCING TIME AND RESPONSIBILITIES

"TO EVERYTHING THERE IS A SEASON,
A TIME FOR EVERY PURPOSE UNDER HEAVEN."

Ecclesiastes 3:1 NKJV

"*P*lease, Mom? Please?" At some time or another, children beg for a pet. They want a puppy, a kitty, or a pony more than anything else in the world. And so they make rash promises. "I'll take care of it! I promise!" But the answering parent invariably uses the R word. "I don't think you're ready for the *responsibility* yet." All the child can see is the idealistic side of pet ownership. They want a pet to cuddle and play with and teach to do clever tricks. All the parent can see is the amount of work inherent with this new responsibility. Where a child sees an adorable puppy, the parent sees vet bills, walks in the rain, and soiled carpeting.

CLEARING ✦ THE ✦ COBWEBS

When you were younger, what did you beg for, only to be told you weren't old enough or responsible enough to take care of it?

What is true with a puppy is true in every area of life. With every new acquisition we make comes the responsibility to keeping it up. This holds true with our use of time. Some things *sound* good at first — signing all the kids up for soccer, joining a book club, teaching a preschool class on Sundays, and volunteering to bake cookies for the third grade bake sale. Sure, there's nothing wrong with any of these things. But with each comes a commitment of time and a shuffling of our other responsibilities. There are never enough hours in the day for all the things we wish we could accomplish. But there is only so much you can physically do in one day. So we have to pick and choose. A balance must be struck between what time we have and what responsibilities fill the hours.

1. Life is short. Time is short. It's a challenge just to finish what we've begun.

Psalm 39:11 — "Surely every man is _____" (NKJV).

Psalm 62:9 — "From the _____ to the _____ — all are _____ in his sight. If you _____ them on the _____, they are _____ than a _____ of _____" (NLT).

James 4:14 — "You do not know what will _____ _____. For what is your _____? It is even a _____ that appears for a _____ _____ and then _____ away" (NKJV).

2. What is the psalmist's poetic description of reaching the end of our days in Psalm 90:9?

3. Paul has an interesting way of urging believers to make the most of their days. What does he tell us to do, both in Ephesians 5:16 and Colossians 4:5?

The most wonderful truth behind dealing with distractions is that we don't need to organize and plan with our natural ability alone. If we yield ourselves to the Holy Spirit, He will order our steps according to His purposes.

Thelma Wells

*V*ery often we think that if we can just get that one, next vital thing we want so badly, our lives will magically fall into balance. "If I could just get that raise." "If we only had two cars." "Once we get this one out of diapers." "If we had a bigger house." If your life seems out of balance now, something more than an external change is needed to get it back in line. I used to think that having a bigger house would help me to be more organized. So, when we moved from a tiny two-bedroom house into a comparatively expansive four-bedroom house, I thought I had it made. So much room. So much potential. So much work! Where I once had just one bathroom to scrub each day, I found myself with three to tidy. The vacuuming that used to take ten minutes now took half an hour. And there were hidden costs, too, like the doubling of most of our utility bills! The thing I thought would make my life simpler actually landed me with more work!

4. Balancing our time and responsibilities may start with looking for lost or wasted time. Instead of shrugging our shoulders and saying, "Where does the time go?" we might need to take a long, careful look at just where our time went! What does Paul tell us the ancient Athenians did to fritter away their days in Acts 17:21?

5. True and False

____ Life is ours to enjoy. There is plenty of time for "religion" later on, after we've had our fun (Mark 13:33).

____ Our time is always ready (John 7:6).

____ Times of refreshing come from the presence of the Lord (Acts 3:19).

____ It's high time we snapped out of it and took notice. The time for which we've been waiting is closer than we thought (Rom. 13:11).

____ We've nothing to worry about and can live as we please, for God has a soft spot in His heart for those of us who mean well (1 Pet. 1:17).

____ We're called to humble ourselves, and that's all. But God, in His own time, may choose to exalt us (1 Pet. 5:6).

As in all arenas of successful living, we attempt to work toward a balance.

Marilyn Meberg

DIGGING DEEPER

Every season of life carries with it different responsibilities. Our lives at age twenty are vastly different from our lives at age forty. Each season may require sacrifices on our parts. Each season carries with it special blessings and joys. This week, instead of digging deeper into the Scriptures, dig around for a while in your heart. What have your hopes been for each season of life? Have you had to set some of them aside for a season? Has God used these seasons to teach you? What have you learned?

PONDER & PRAY

This week ponder over your responsibilities. Do you have too many for the time you have? None of us wants to look back with regret for the time we squandered on unimportant things. Pray for uncommon clarity in seeing the things that truly matter. Pray for the courage to take on responsibilities that will require much of you. And in equal measure, pray for the courage to say no to the things that tax your time and energy to no good purpose.

TRINKET TO TREASURE

Your trinket this week is a small token to remind you to think long and hard before taking on responsibilities for which you may not have the time—a dog collar. Puppies may bring us great delight, but we must be willing to give them the care and attention they need. Even so, we are offered many an enticing opportunity in our days. We are the ones who must choose how those days are spent. We must balance the time we have with the responsibilities we take on.

✦ NOTES & PRAYER REQUESTS ✦

✦ Notes & Prayer Requests ✦

CHAPTER 3

BALANCING SCHEDULES AND INTERRUPTIONS

"HE TOLD THEM, 'YOU DON'T GET TO KNOW THE TIME.
TIMING IS THE FATHER'S BUSINESS.'"

Acts 1:7 MSG

One of literature's quirkier characters is the English gentleman Phileas Fogg. He with his top hat, pocket watch, and valet Passepartout, appear in Jules Verne's classic book, *Around the World in Eighty Days*. Phileas Fogg leads a carefully structured life. Every minute of his day is accounted for, down to the slightest detail. "Tea and toast at twenty-three minutes past eight, the shaving-water at thirty-seven minutes past nine . . . . Everything was regulated and foreseen that was to be done from half-past eleven A.M. till

CLEARING + THE + COBWEBS

Who is one of your favorite characters from literature? Why does this character appeal to you?

midnight, the hour at which the methodical gentleman retired." Fogg ate the same meals on each day of the week. He let his valet know the exact temperature his shaving-water should be—eighty-six degrees. The other gentlemen in his club could set their watch by his arrival each morning. Every aspect of Phileas Fogg's large house was organized, from cellars to attic. Clean, neat, and regular. This was not the kind of man to have a junk drawer in his kitchen or piles of clutter in his closets. "Mr. Fogg's wardrobe was amply supplied and in the best taste. Each pair of trousers, coat, and vest bore a number, indicating the time of year and season at which they were in turn to be laid out for wearing; and the same system was applied to the master's shoes." Phileas Fogg took great pride and satisfaction in being as regular as clockwork, uninterrupted by the world around him.

Generally, we can't manage the same regularity in our lives. Even when our intentions are good, we're foiled by the unexpected. Distractions, interruptions, complications. There's always some unforeseen hitch to our plans.

1. Some women are just more organized than others. I've known women who've attempted to schedule their daily routines down to the quarter of every hour! But the best-laid plans of mice and men are forever being interrupted! What do Psalm 33:10, 11 and Proverbs 19:21 remind us about our scheming and schedules?

2. When we have our eyes fixed on our own plans, we see every interruption to them as an irritation and an inconvenience. But what does Proverbs 16:9 tell us God is doing?

3. When it comes to balancing our schedules with the interruptions that constantly block our best intentions, what does Philippians 2:13 urge us to remember?

> *I realized how tart I become when inconvenienced. It doesn't take much of a breeze to topple me. I want to believe that, if called upon to be a heroine, I would rise to the occasion. But experience has proven me feeble.*
>
> Patsy Clairmont

4. We cannot always understand God's working in our lives. He does things in unexpected and often incomprehensible ways! Why does Isaiah 55:8, 9 say we are so puzzled over God's plans?

Our world is governed by certain physical laws. They have been discovered and explained by men and women of science through the years. But far more famous, though decidedly unscientific, is Murphy's Law. Have you heard of it? Murphy's Law states, "If anything can go wrong, it will." We have days and weeks and months when Murphy's Law seems to be the reigning force in our lives. Nothing goes as we expected or intended. But as Christians, we need to cling to the fact that God is at work in our lives, and His purposes are always served. <u>What seems a mistake to our way of thinking might be just the thing God can use for His glory in our lives.</u>

5. What does Romans 11:33 compare God's ways with?

6. God tells us that His ways are higher than our ways—beyond our ability to understand. But does that mean we shouldn't even try to grasp them? What does Scripture tell us about our ways and God's ways?

____ Deuteronomy 10:12   a. We should delight in knowing God's ways.

____ Isaiah 2:3   b. "Show me Your ways, O LORD."

____ Isaiah 58:2   c. The LORD ponders all our paths.

____ Daniel 5:23   d. The LORD will teach us His ways.

____ Psalm 25:4   e. God owns all our ways.

____ Psalm 145:17   f. We should examine our own ways.

____ Proverbs 5:21   g. God requires us to walk in His ways.

____ Lamentations 3:40   h. The LORD is righteous in all His ways.

7. When we search for balance between our schedules and the interruptions that interfere with them, we must calm our frustrated heart and remind ourselves that it is God who directs our days.

• What does Jeremiah 10:23 tell us is not in us to control?

• What does the psalmist pray will direct his steps in Psalm 119:133?

There are occasions when my perfectly laid plans don't work for me. Why? Interruptions! Unexpected delays. Circumstances out of my control. That's when I have to make a choice— either lose my mind (and my decorum!), or look beyond my puny plan and see if God has something different or even better in store.

Luci Swindoll

8. We can experience an attitude adjustment when we realize that our very schedules are in God's hands. Instead of groaning over inconveniences, we should be watching for opportunities in them and trusting God for the outcomes. What is Paul's prayer for us in 2 Thessalonians 3:5?

DIGGING DEEPER

Think back over the Bible stories you are most familiar with. Do you think that these men and women were immediately aware of God's sovereign plans when their lives were rather rudely interrupted?

- Joseph went from coddled son to foreign slave.
- Moses went from wealthy prince to humble shepherd.
- Ruth went from new bride to young widow.
- David went from trusted shield-bearer to public enemy number one.
- Esther went from beauty queen to spokeswoman for her whole race.
- Daniel went from trusted advisor to death row inmate.
- Mary went from bride-to-be to the brunt of local gossip.

PONDER & PRAY

Though evidence may seem to the contrary, Murphy's Law does not reign in our lives. When everything seems to be going wrong, we needn't become frustrated or discouraged. Pray for the spiritual awareness to see interruptions as just one more part of God's sovereign plan for your day! This week, consider how this unique perspective changes your attitude about interruptions.

TRINKET TO TREASURE

Though we may try, as Phileas Fogg did, to schedule our lives down to the smallest detail, we are bound to face interruptions. Our trinket this week is a pocket watch—perfect for those of us with a penchant for punctuality. But our plans are no match for God's purposes, and we are often stopped in our tracks by some unexpected turn of events. When you're interrupted, and your first reaction is one of irritation at the inconvenience, check the time on your watch and check your attitude. Our plans may be inconvenienced, but God's plans are right on schedule. There may be something in this interruption that He will use for His glory! Trust Him to direct your ways.

✦ NOTES & PRAYER REQUESTS ✦

CHAPTER 4

BALANCING WORK AND REST

"GO TO THE ANT, YOU SLUGGARD! CONSIDER HER WAYS AND BE WISE."

Proverbs 6:6 NKJV

*I*n one of Aesop's most familiar fables, we are introduced to the ants and the grasshopper. The ants, industrious fellows, work all through the summer months. They're not the sort to linger for gossip at the water cooler and take long lunch breaks. Nope. These critters are focused on the task at hand. They are determined to bring in their harvest and store it away before the first frost. If they're able to store away enough food, they'll be comfortable during the cold months ahead. But the grasshopper is a fun-loving creature, fiddling and dancing his summer days away. Why worry? Why sweat? He lives for the moment, and enjoys each summer day without thought

CLEARING ✦ THE ✦ COBWEBS

If you could indulge in a lazy day, without any responsibilities, what would you most like to do?

33

for tomorrow. So when the bitter cold of winter comes, he has no food or shelter because he did not plan ahead.

With the handiness of local grocery stores, few of us have to put up summer produce to last us through the winter anymore. But the principle of diligence will always be timely. Solomon condemns the lazy, the slothful, and the sluggard in no uncertain terms. But on the other hand Scripture brings to our attention the vital place of rest in our days. And so we are left to strike the balance. How much work is too much work? How much rest is too much rest? Where is the balance?

1. The moral of Aesop's fable is not far from the proverb of Solomon. Scripture scorns the lazy person as a fool. There are many proverbs which deal harshly with the slothful and the sluggards!

___ Proverbs 6:9	a. The lazy man won't even cook what he's caught.
___ Proverbs 12:24	b. The way of the lazy is like a hedge of thorns.
___ Proverbs 12:27	c. The lazy man will be forced to work.
___ Proverbs 13:4	d. The lazy man's hands refuse to labor.
___ Proverbs 15:19	e. How long will you slumber, O sluggard?
___ Proverbs 21:25	f. The lazy man desires, but has nothing.

2. Even in New Testament times, laziness was not tolerated. What was Paul's firm admonition in 2 Thessalonians 3:10?

3. Though "Idle hands are the devil's playground," we are also fond of saying, "All work and no play makes Jack a dull boy." Rest and recreation have their place in our lives. In fact, God commands it! What was His established weekly routine according to Exodus 23:12 and Exodus 31:15?

We don't always have time for grand departures to wonderful retreats or resorts where we can be refreshed and renewed. That is why I treasure small harbors. They are all around us waiting to let us catch our breath before the next wind carries us away.

Sheila Walsh

*Y*es, hard workers are admired for their diligence. But God knew the importance of balanced living, and so He built in times of rest for His people. We are all familiar with the Sabbath day of rest, which was strictly enforced throughout Israel. But did you know that there were also prescribed festivals on every Jewish calendar? Three times a year all God's people were expected to set aside their labor and converge on Jerusalem. These were times of worship, of reunion, of fellowship, and of feasting.

4. Sometimes our responsibilities have a way of piling up around us, leaving us stressed out and ready for escape. Has your heart ever echoed the psalmist's prayer in Psalm 55:6?

5. There are times when we need to face up to our responsibilities, buckle down and see them through. But there are also times when we need a rest.

• What practical need of the disciples was Jesus willing to address in Mark 6:31?

• What does Jesus promise to those who will come to Him in Matthew 11:28, 29?

6. Work and rest must be kept in balance. Too much rest comes down to laziness, and too much work can burn us out. In Scripture, the middle-ground we seek can be found in the word *diligence.*

Proverbs 27:23 — Be diligent to _____.

2 Timothy 2:15 — Be diligent to _____.

Hebrews 4:11 — Be diligent to _____.

2 Peter 1:10 — Be diligent to _____.

2 Peter 3:14 — Be diligent to _____.

7. "A little sleep, a little slumber, A little folding of the hands to rest" (Prov. 24:33 NKJV), and our whole world can fall apart! What does Solomon urge us to do in Proverbs 4:23?

DIGGING DEEPER

Diligence is a thread that runs through all of Scripture. We are wise when we take care of what is ours diligently. We are foolish when we are lazy and neglect the things in our care. Here are just a few more passages that urge us on to diligence in our hearts and lives.

- Romans 12:11
- 2 Corinthians 8:7
- Hebrews 6:11
- 2 Peter 1:5

PONDER & PRAY

Every life needs a balance of work and rest. Too much of either is bad for body and soul. This week, pray for wisdom in understanding which you need and when. Ask God for a diligent heart, willing to take on the task at hand. But ask the Lord to show you the healthy place rest can have in your life. When work and rest are in proper balance, you'll be whole, hale, and hearty!

TRINKET TO TREASURE

Solomon did well in urging us to consider the ants, so this week's trinket simply must be an ant! These little critters are admirable in their ability to work steadily, with due diligence. Hard workers are praised in the proverbs, just as the lazy sluggards are condemned. So our ants will urge us to get our work done, but let us not forget that work must be balanced by rest. Let times of rest refresh your hearts and bodies, just as God intended.

✦ NOTES & PRAYER REQUESTS ✦

CHAPTER 5

BALANCING FAITH AND SIGHT

"FOR BY HIM ALL THINGS WERE CREATED THAT ARE IN HEAVEN AND THAT ARE ON EARTH, VISIBLE AND INVISIBLE."

Colossians 1:16 NKJV

One of the most fascinating news stories I've ever heard emerged on *National Public Radio* as they followed a reporter into an unusual restaurant. As you enter the restaurant's foyer, daylight is replaced by dimness. Before your eyes have a chance to adjust, it's time to follow your hostess back to your table. Winding your way deeper into the restaurant, you are plunged into total darkness. There is no glimmer of light. You cannot see the hand in front of your face. The blackness is complete. Many guests find this sensory deprivation unnerving. You cannot read the menu. You cannot see the food placed before you. You cannot see your dinner

CLEARING ✦ THE ✦ COBWEBS

What kinds of games did you play growing up that were best played in the dark?

companions. Yet orders are taken, and food is prepared, and waiters and waitresses find their way through the blackness with unerring confidence. Why? Because they're blind. The restaurant is run by the local school for the blind, and their unique dining phenomenon allows a seeing populace the brief experience of living with blindness. These patrons never saw the inside of that restaurant. They couldn't tell you the color of the walls or the pattern on the tablecloths. They couldn't tell you what their waitress looked like, or how their plates were garnished. But the fact that they couldn't see all of these things didn't mean those things weren't there. They put their trust in hosts they could not see to take care of their needs during the course of their meal.

We, too, live by faith and not by sight.

1. What does Paul tell us that creation points to in Romans 1:20?

> *We can talk to the One who is able to calm our apprehensions and fears and give us courage to move ahead with a heart of confidence and assurance.*
>
> Luci Swindoll

2. Creation is not the only evidence that stands to testify of God's presence. What does Psalm 145:4 say can point to God's power with confidence?

It is easy to believe that God can use our lives when we see immediate results, when positive feedback encourages us to push on. It is hard to keep walking when we see little sign that what we are doing is making a difference.

Sheila Walsh

3. What does Colossians 1:16 tell us about creation?

*T*here are many children's games that require us to blindfold our eyes and rely on our other senses to get along. The earliest of such games is pin the tail on the donkey. With a bandana or dishcloth wound across our faces, we were spun around in circles until it was hard to stand up straight. Disoriented and confused, we were gently pushed in the right direction, our hands extended and steps slowed by uncertainty. As we got older, we were taught how to play blind man's bluff and Marco Polo. Each requiring the player who is "it" to cover their eyes.

Christianity requires many of us to ignore the evidence of our eyes. Instead, we learn to rely on other senses to navigate. We trust an unseen God to gently push us in the right direction. We tune our ears to the Spirit's promptings. We walk according to the wisdom of the Word. We put our trust in unseen realities.

4. What unseen thing did Job ask after, according to Job 17:15?

5. How does Hebrews 11:1 describe the relationship between our faith and our hope?

6. What does 2 Corinthians 5:7 tell us is vital to our way of life—our walk?

> *Prayer isn't magic. Jesus did not come to make our suffering disappear in an instant. Instead He came to fill it with His presence.*
>
> Barbara Johnson

7. There is enough *seen* in this world to encourage us in our faith in the unseen. But faith requires us to trust in God. We depend upon Him to bring all of His promises and our hopes to pass.

• What is the staunch declaration of Psalm 31:14?

• What two other things besides trusting does Psalm 73:28 tell of?

DIGGING DEEPER

Our own faith is encouraged by tangible things—the wonders of creation and the testimonies of fellow believers. Another source of strong faith is found in answered prayers. They assure us that God hears us and answers us in our times of need.
• Psalm 10:17
• Psalm 77:1
• Isaiah 65:24

PONDER & PRAY

Thomas, a disciple of Jesus, declared that he would not believe in the risen Lord unless he could see Jesus with his own eyes and touch Him with his own hands. We do not have the benefit of Thomas's face-to-face encounter with Christ. But we are not left to a truly "blind" faith. With every year that passes, archeology continues to uncover more evidence to confirm the validity of Scripture's history. This week, ponder the things that ground our faith, and the things that we must take by faith.

TRINKET TO TREASURE

The Christian walk is hardly a game of blind man's bluff, and yet we place enormous trust in things we cannot see. Our trinket for this week is a blindfold. For as believers, we must often mistrust the evidence of our eyes and give preference to those things that can only be held by faith. We trust in an invisible God. We await a Savior we cannot see. We cling to a hope whose only evidence is our faith. "We walk by faith, not by sight" (2 Cor. 5:7 NKJV).

✦ Notes & Prayer Requests ✦

CHAPTER 6

BALANCING LOVE AND OBEDIENCE

"IF YOU LOVE ME, KEEP MY COMMANDMENTS."

John 14:15 NKJV

*S*ad to say, many a young wife has tried to have her own way by unscrupulous means. Even the daintiest little woman knows how to throw her weight around. The pouting lip. The trembling chin. The tears that threaten to spill over. And with a slightly sulky tone of voice, the words few young husbands can stand up to: "If you *really* loved me, you would . . ." Each of us could fill in that blank a little differently. *You would bring me flowers. You would listen to me when I talk. You would fix the garbage disposal. You would take me out for dinner once in a while. You would know what I'm thinking. You would let me buy a new sofa.* The list of our reasonable and unreasonable expectations could be endless.

CLEARING ✦ THE ✦ COBWEBS

What is the strangest thing you were ever dared to do? Did you go through with it?

Shame on all of us for being manipulative little minxes. But even in our efforts to hold sway over our husbands, we *did* get one fact straight. "If you really loved me, you would . . ." Real love is demonstrated. It's expressed somehow. It's shown by word and deed. Jesus said as much to His disciples. "If you love Me, keep My commandments" (John 14:15 NKJV). It's the deeds that prove the love. They point to its existence.

1. Love is displayed. It's recognizable. It is demonstrated in tangible ways. Even God demonstrated His love for us. What does Paul tell us God did in Romans 5:8?

2. We, too, are expected to demonstrate our love for God. How does Deuteronomy 11:1 suggest we show our love for the Lord?

3. What's the use of a parent who tells their child, "Do as I say, not as I do"? We cannot claim to believe something if we don't put it into practice. What condemnation did God bring down on those who seemed to honor Him outwardly, according to Isaiah 29:13?

*E*ven grade-schoolers know that talk is cheap. Anyone can brag over their accomplishments and boast of their intentions. But admiration must be earned by solid evidence. So the age-old challenge echoes across every schoolyard. "Oh yeah? Prove it!"

4. John, the beloved disciple, has a clear-cut perspective on what love is and how it affects our lives.

John 14:24 — "He who does not _____ Me does not _____ My _____" (NKJV).

John 15:10 — "If you _____ My commandments, you will _____ in My _____, just as I have _____ My Father's commandments and _____ in His _____" (NKJV).

5. Love isn't an ideal or a daydream or a castle in the air. Love is so very practical. Love is hands-on. Love rolls up its sleeves and proves itself.

• What was the promise God made in Deuteronomy 7:9?

• How was that promise echoed in prayer in Nehemiah 1:5?

The more I investigated God's love through the Scriptures the more I relaxed; the safety of His love untied the knot of anxiety and perfectionism within me.

Patsy Clairmont

6. Love and obedience go hand in hand. But John reassures us of something encouraging. What does he tell us about God's commandments in 1 John 5:3?

7. What does Jesus promise to do in John 14:23?

DIGGING DEEPER

If you want a really clear picture of just how love and obedience fit together, take a plunge into the Book of 1 John. Read it right through—it's only five chapters long. John, the beloved disciple, doesn't pull any punches. The directness of this little book will take your breath away!

PONDER & PRAY

This week, pray that God would give you a fresh understanding of how love and obedience are intertwined. Have you ever considered how many ways we can show love for one another? Ponder through the practical aspects of loving, and maybe even start a list! How can we demonstrate our love for God?

TRINKET TO TREASURE

You've heard of tying a bit of string around one finger as a reminder? Well this week's trinket is just such a bit of string, but we'll tie it around the finger! Why? Because this week we must keep in mind that love doesn't mean manipulating someone so that they're wrapped around your finger. We should not say, "If you *really* loved me you would . . ." But love *is* demonstrated by our actions. That's why Jesus said, "If you love Me, keep My commandments" (John 14:15 NKJV).

✦ NOTES & PRAYER REQUESTS ✦

CHAPTER 7

BALANCING FAITH AND WORKS

"AND LET OUR PEOPLE ALSO LEARN TO MAINTAIN GOOD WORKS, TO MEET URGENT NEEDS, THAT THEY MAY NOT BE UNFRUITFUL."

Titus 3:14 NKJV

My father-in-law was a history teacher for many years, and from him we inherited several antiquated maps. These are prints of beautiful, old maps that had been drawn up during the early days of the exploration of the New World. The known world was drawn with confidence and in some detail, but where strange, uncharted regions were mapped, the lines became vague, uncertain, and often inaccurate. Yet these were all the ships' captains had to go by. Out of necessity, they trusted these charts when plotting their courses. Nowadays, we have superior maps, based on satellite imagery and linked to Internet search engines. All you

CLEARING ✦ THE ✦ COBWEBS

Have you ever been the victim of a practical joke? Or better yet, have you ever pulled one? What was it?

have to do is type in your starting point and the address of your destination, and a computer will generate driving directions.

But a map only does us good if we trust it and follow its directions. Our family has always enjoyed the tradition of the Sunday afternoon drive, and we've often set off into the countryside with no real idea of where we're trying to get to. We jokingly tell people that we try to get ourselves lost, just to see if we can find our way home again. On one particular Sunday afternoon, we were well and truly lost. We drove back and forth, hoping to intersect a familiar road, but to no avail. The only highway we crossed was unfamiliar to us, so we dug in the glove compartment for a map and attempted to chart our position. Much to our astonishment, the highway we'd crossed and re-crossed was the very road we needed—the very road we lived off of—but it had changed names across county lines. With accurate bearings from the map, we confidently turned our faces homeward.

There's a big difference between having a map in the glove box and relying on that map for direction. It's the difference between believing in the map's accuracy and acting upon it. Believing and acting. What we say and what we do. That's the difference between faith and works.

1. The balance between faith and works is one of those longstanding controversies of Christianity. Why? Because at first glance, Scripture seems to contradict itself.

• What does Paul say justifies us in Galatians 2:16?

• What does James say justifies us in James 2:24?

2. Why are works so pivotal in a life of faith, according to Titus 1:16?

3. Throughout his letter to believers, James challenges believers to walk their talk!

James 2:14 — "What does it _____, my brethren, if someone _____ he has _____ but does not have _____? Can _____ _____ him?" (NKJV).

James 2:17 — "Thus also faith _____ _____, if it does not have _____, is _____" (NKJV).

James 2:18 — "But someone will say, 'You have _____, and I have _____.' _____ _____ your faith _____ your works, and I will _____ _____ my faith _____ my works" (NKJV).

4. How does James describe faith without works in James 2:20 and James 2:26?

The wonderful thing about the Christian life is that we all enter freely. No matter who you are, where you're from, what your experience has been, Jesus Christ invites you to freely come. No conditions. No restrictions. No small print. No waiting. About this, you can be certain.

Luci Swindoll

5. So is James really saying that faith is unnecessary for salvation? No, of course not. But what does James 2:22 tell us that our works do for our faith?

6. Let's take a step back and look at faith and works from a little different perspective. According to Ephesians 2:10, why were we created?

7. Even Paul, Mr. Justification-by-Faith, understood the vital place of good works in the life of believers. Just look at his words to Timothy and Titus.

___ 1 Timothy 5:25	a. God's people are zealous for good works.
___ 1 Timothy 6:18	b. Show yourself to be a pattern of good works.
___ Titus 2:7	c. The good works of some are clearly evident.
___ Titus 2:14	d. Be careful to maintain good works.
___ Titus 3:8	e. Let them be rich in good works.

8. For those who want to balance faith and works in their lives, the New Testament points in the right direction.

- How does James 3:13 say those who are wise will behave themselves?

- What does Titus 3:14 say we need to learn?

- What do we need to do in order to stir up good works, according to Hebrews 10:24?

9. What are the good works in our lives able to accomplish according to Matthew 5:16 and 1 Peter 2:12?

Digging Deeper

Frequently in Scripture, we find that it's the women who are doing good works. The Proverbs 31 woman is the ultimate gracious lady, but here are a few other passages from which we can learn.

- Acts 9:36
- 1 Timothy 2:10
- 1 Timothy 5:10

Ponder & Pray

This week, take a look around you and give some thought as to the good you can do. Pray for perceptiveness as you consider those around you. Watch for opportunities to be a helper, a comforter, and an encourager. Pray that the Spirit will stir up your desire to do good works. Ask for the strength to maintain good works. And keep in mind that the good we do is not for our own bolstered reputation, but for the glory of God. All we do can point others to Him!

TRINKET TO TREASURE

Your trinket this week is a map. Just as a road map only does us any good if we believe in its accuracy and follow its directions, our faith only does anyone any good if we do something with it. What we say we believe must match up with what we do. Our actions give testimony to a faith that is otherwise invisible.

✦ NOTES & PRAYER REQUESTS ✦

BALANCING WANTS AND NEEDS

"AND GOD WILL GENEROUSLY PROVIDE ALL YOU NEED. THEN YOU WILL ALWAYS HAVE EVERYTHING YOU NEED AND PLENTY LEFT OVER TO SHARE WITH OTHERS."

2 Corinthians 9:8 NLT

Color is very important to me. Perhaps my eye for color is inherited from my mother, who is an artist. I can always tell when a red has too much of an orange to it, or a green has a yellow cast. I like things to match exactly, and have a tendency to decorate in monochromatic schemes—the colors always the same, but in varying patterns and textures. I actually carry paint swatches around in my purse, so that I can compare the colors of items I run across in stores with the actual colors I have painted my walls. Not long ago, my longsuffering husband played chauffer on my search for a new shower curtain for the upstairs

CLEARING
✦ THE ✦
COBWEBS

What's the longest you've had to hunt for that perfect *something*? How many stores did you have to go through before finding something that suited?

bathroom. I had to go through seven different stores before finding the perfect match. In the grand scheme of things, does it really matter if my shower curtain is just the same color as the painted walls? No. As my husband blandly pointed out, I could have made due with any old liner. I didn't *need* the perfect shower curtain—sheer navy with delicate white embroidery—but, oh, how I *wanted* it!

1. One of God's names is *Jehovah Jireh*, the God Who Provides. It should be a comfort to know that the One who knows just what we need is the very One who provides for those needs.

Genesis 22:14 — "And Abraham called the name of the place _____; as it is said to this day, 'In the Mount of the LORD it shall be _____'" (NKJV).

Psalm 65:9 — "You _____ the earth and _____ it, You greatly _____ it; The river of God is full of water; You _____ their grain, For so You have _____ it" (NKJV).

2. When does God know when we're in need, according to Matthew 6:8?

3. Is God stingy in His provision for us? What does Paul say in 2 Corinthians 9:8?

4. What does God's abundant provision free us from, according to Luke 12:29?

*G*rowing up, one of the biggest events of the weeks leading up to Christmas was the arrival of the Sears Christmas catalog. For weeks my sister and I would pour over its pages, pointing out the merits of this toy and that toy. We'd each choose our favorites, and imagine what it would be like to actually receive them. Even today, I enjoy getting catalogs—I get dozens of them! Since I can't get out shopping very often, I let my catalogs pile up until some rainy day, then settle in for a long, luxurious browse. By the end, I've got a pile filled with dog-eared pages and sticky-note markers. All sorts of things catch my eye—this dress or that set of dishes or a delightful new cake pan. But in the end, I rarely send for those items. In the end, I decide they're more *wants* than *needs*.

5. When the number of our *wants* tips our life out of balance, we are easily overrun by greed, covetousness, and the urge to accumulate things we really don't need. What does Ephesians 5:5 compare greed with?

6. Earthly treasure passes away. It's worthless in the face of eternity. So Jesus tells us to seek eternal treasures—the ones we will find waiting for us in heaven.

____ Psalm 119:162   a. Heaven is worth trading everything to get.

____ Matthew 13:44   b. God's power is a precious treasure.

____ Mark 10:21   c. Gold and silver have become worthless.

____ Luke 12:34   d. I rejoice at Your word as one who finds great treasure.

____ 2 Corinthians 4:7   e. Sell all your worldly stuff for heavenly treasure.

____ James 5:3   f. Wherever your treasure is, there your heart is

7. What do each of these verses tell us is real treasure—the sort of thing we really do need?

• 1 Timothy 6:19

• Job 22:25

DIGGING DEEPER

One of the character qualities God loves to see in His children is generosity. "So let each one give as he purposes in his heart, not grudgingly or of necessity; for God loves a cheerful giver" (2 Cor. 9:7 NKJV). What do each of these verses tell us about the generous at heart?
• Psalm 37:21
• Psalm 112:5
• Proverbs 11:25
• Proverbs 22:9
• Isaiah 32:8
• 2 Corinthians 9:13

PONDER & PRAY

God assures us that we will have everything we need. Give some thought this week to your level of contentment. Are you confident in God's ability to provide for you? Do greedy thoughts sometimes overtake your better sense? Pray this week for a genuinely thankful heart. Ask the Lord to show you just how many of your needs He has seen to. And pray, also, for a generous heart, willing to give when you have more than you need.

TRINKET TO TREASURE

Your trinket this week is an everlasting reminder of the battle between *wants* and *needs*. Paint swatches help me to find the perfect match, though in the process I pass over many things that could have made do just as well. Sometimes, God gives us just what we wanted—and those times can be delightful. But other times, He asks us to make do with what's on hand—which can make it hard to be grateful. When our longing for the wants in life seem to overwhelm us, we can keep in mind that all this stuff passes away. God knows just what we need, and He's provided the perfect match. God Himself is what we need, and He will be our treasure.

CHAPTER 9

BALANCING LONGING AND CONTENTMENT

"AND HAVING FOOD AND CLOTHING, WITH THESE WE SHALL BE CONTENT."

1 Timothy 6:8 NKJV

rowing up, I remember seeing several game shows on television. Lazy summer days could be whiled away in front of such fare as *The Price is Right, Tic Tac Toe, The Joker's Wild,* and *Family Feud.* One of the most fascinating game shows I ever saw was called *Let's Make a Deal.* In this game, contestants were chosen from the audience and asked to make tough choices. The game show host, Monty Hall, would count out crisp dollar bills into some giddy gal's hand, then ask her the fatal question. "Do you want to keep that $500 for yourself, or trade it in for what's behind door number two?" It was hard to let go of

CLEARING ✦ THE ✦ COBWEBS

Do you have a favorite game show—past or present?

some prizes—watches, recliners, toaster ovens. But the thought of something bigger and better would coax newly-won prizes out of their hands. "Do you want to keep that shiny new camera, or trade it in for what's under box number three?" Sometimes contestants would win even bigger—a cruise, a car, a substantial cash prize. And the hope of that something better would make that thing in their hand seem small and insignificant in comparison.

I think we are often tempted to make light of what we have when we suspect there is something better to be had. Why be content with a blender when there might be a diamond tiara behind curtain number one? And this attitude carries over into everyday things. If I only had a newer car, a bigger house, a nicer neighborhood, a bigger paycheck, a different mother-in-law, a smaller dress size, a more considerate husband . . . then I would be happy! But would that really make us content, or would we drop it in hopes that the next deal we make will be even better?

Why do we so often feel that "there's something better out there"? I believe we're often uncomfortable with ourselves, so we go outside ourselves in search of someone, something, or some place that will bring us contentment.

Luci Swindoll

1. Restlessness. Longing. Dissatisfaction. As wonderful as this life can be, there is always some feeling of something missing. How did Solomon sum up this attitude in Ecclesiastes 1:2?

2. Most of the time, we consider lack of satisfaction a bad thing! Miserliness, materialism, greed all come from wanting what we don't have.

Ecclesiastes 1:8 — "The _____ is not _____ with _____, Nor the _____ _____ with _____" (NKJV).

Proverbs 30:15, 16 — "The _____ has two _____-_____ and _____! There are three things that are never _____, Four never say, '_____!': The _____, The _____ _____, The _____ that is not satisfied with _____—And the _____ never says, '_____!'" (NKJV).

Ecclesiastes 5:10 — "He who _____ _____ will not be _____ with _____; Nor he who _____ _____, with _____. This also is _____" (NKJV).

3. But strangely enough, not all of our longings and discontentment are for bad reasons.

• What does David long for, according to Psalm 84:2?

• What intense longing does the psalmist speak of in Psalm 119:20?

4. What longing can only be satisfied by God, according to Psalm 107:9?

There's an old proverb well worth remembering: "A bird in the hand is worth two in the bush." What does that mean? Think of it this way. Which would you rather have—the possibility of doubling your money with the risk of coming up empty-handed, or the certainty of hanging onto the sum you hold in your hand? What's the use of two birds in the bush? Sure, there are two of them, but they're not yours unless you catch them both. It's better to have one that's good and caught than to long for those that are more plentiful, but out of your reach.

Are you content to do without and make do? Are you content to bloom where you're planted? Are you content with the bird in your hand?

5. Paul knew all about doing without. What is his familiar claim in Philippians 4:11?

You were made for more than this world has to offer you. Our yearnings, longings, cravings, and hopes are telling us something: there isn't enough love, peace, hope, friendship, and intimacy on this earth to completely satisfy us. We will always want more.

Nicole Johnson

6. What did Paul consider to be great gain, according to 1 Timothy 6:6?

7. Why does Hebrews 13:5 say that we can be content?

8. The truth of the matter is, we will never be completely satisfied this side of heaven. That restlessness and longing in our souls is for God, and until we see Him, it will remain. People have always looked forward to that day. What do each of these verses speak about?

• Job 19:25–27

• 1 Corinthians 13:12

DIGGING DEEPER

Longing and contentment are difficult to balance. On the one hand, we should be content with what God gives us. But on the other hand, we should never be satisfied with the things of this world. A part of us will always long for God and heaven. On the contentment side, here are a few verses extolling the quiet life. And on the longing side, a few verses reminding us where our satisfaction must come from.

• 1 Thessalonians 4:11
• 1 Timothy 2:2
• 1 Peter 3:4
• Psalm 36:8
• Psalm 65:4
• Proverbs 14:14

PONDER & PRAY

This week's prayers should seek that delicate balance between longing and contentment. Ask the Lord for grace to be content where He has placed you and with the blessings He has given you. Perhaps you can emulate Paul, in his determination to be content no matter what your circumstances may be. And balance this out at the same time, by listening to that quiet yearning in your heart. Does your soul long for heaven?

TRINKET TO TREASURE

The old saying goes, "A bird in the hand is worth two in the bush." And so this week's trinket is a bird in the hand. We don't need to look beyond what God has given us, always striving for the next, big thing. Balancing longing and contentment comes when we learn to be thankful for what God has given us, and when we learn that complete satisfaction won't really be ours until we're in glory.

✦ Notes & Prayer Requests ✦

CHAPTER 10

BALANCING UNITY AND DIVERSITY

"BEHOLD, HOW GOOD AND HOW PLEASANT IT IS FOR BRETHREN TO DWELL TOGETHER IN UNITY!"

Psalm 133:1 NKJV

I have a little flock of parakeets in my family room—five bright little birds of a feather. Keeping them has been a delight. Their needs are simple—fresh water and filled seed cups. Their cheerful chattering, twittering, and chorusing are a part of what makes home feel homey. When they first came to live with us, it took the better part of two weeks to settle names on them all. Part of the problem was figuring out who was who. They look rather similar to one another. Three of the little birds are white with pale markings, and two are pure yellow. But after watching them for a while, their differences start to become apparent. This little male is pure white. That female

CLEARING
✦ THE ✦
COBWEBS

Have you ever known identical twins? Could you tell them apart? How?

has a turquoise blush to her wings, while the other's tint is almost lavender. One yellow budgie has spots on her wingtips, while the other has a greenish tinge to her underbelly. By focusing on how the parakeets were different from one another, we were able to distinguish them from one another.

People like to stand apart from one another. We like to express our individuality, to set ourselves apart from the crowd, to be ourselves. Because of this, we tend to notice how we're different from one another. And by focusing on those differences, we're able to distinguish ourselves. But as Christians, we're urged not to concentrate on the differences, but on the things that make us the same. In the midst of all our diversity, God calls us to unity!

1. Each and every person has been "fearfully and wonderfully made" by God's own hand. What does Job call himself in Job 10:8?

God made you in His image for His glory. Use your uniqueness to edify people and glorify God. Capitalize on the abilities God has given you. Don't expect other people to be like you or to always understand you. They're busy being uniquely themselves.

Thelma Wells

2. And yet, each one of us is a part of something bigger. How does Paul describe this in Romans 12:5?

3. And what is the proper working of the members of this body, according to 1 Corinthians 1:10?

4. An interesting analogy is used when describing the way the smaller parts must work together for the proper working of the whole. It's mentioned in each of these verses. Can you catch the thread?

- Ephesians 4:16

- Colossians 2:2

- Colossians 2:19

5. Each of us holds a unique place within God's family. But while no one else can quite take our place, neither can any of us do without each other. How does Paul put it in Romans 12:4, 5?

*I*t's a quality we applaud from the time a child is young. Barney sings, "You are different, you're the only one, you're the only one like you! There's no one else in the whole wide world who can do the thing you do! Because you're special, special! Everyone is special! Everyone in his or her own way . . . ." We are assured that we are special because we are unique. No two people are just alike. We're as unique as the snowflakes, unduplicated in spite of the sheer number of us. Our looks vary, we think differently, we have unique traits, preferences, gifts, and quirks. And yet in God's eyes, we all fit together neatly. We balance each other!

6. We're quite certain that "it takes all kinds," but often fail to ask ourselves, "to do what?" When it comes to unity and diversity, what does Paul want us to understand? Look over these verses from *The Message*, and draw your conclusions.

> *"A body isn't just a single part blown up into something huge. It's all the different-but-similar parts arranged and functioning together."* —1 Corinthians 12:14 MSG

Living a Life of Balance

"As it is, we see that God has carefully placed each part of the body right where he wanted it." —1 Corinthians 12:18 MSG

"What we have is one body with many parts, each its proper size and in its proper place. No part is important on its own." —1 Corinthians 12:20 MSG

"You are Christ's body—that's who you are! You must never forget this. Only as you accept your part of that body does your 'part' mean anything." —1 Corinthians 12:27 MSG

7. And suddenly, we look around and realize that we are a part of "one another," and we are called to do much on each other's behalf. What does each of these passages urge us to do for one another?

John 13:34 —

Romans 12:10 —

Romans 15:7 —

1 Corinthians 12:25 —

Galatians 5:13 —

Galatians 6:2 —

Ephesians 4:32 —

1 Thessalonians 5:11 —

Hebrews 3:13 —

James 5:16 —

1 Peter 3:8 —

1 Peter 4:9 —

1 Peter 4:10 —

8. What does Psalm 133:1 declare to be the ultimate "good thing"?

DIGGING DEEPER

There is a balance between unity and diversity. And while most of the New Testament strives to get us to understand that we must work together as believers, there will always be a longing in our heart to know that God knows who we are as individuals. Part of the thrill of one day "knowing as we are known" is the very fact that we are known!

- Psalm 139:1
- John 15:10
- 1 Corinthians 3:8
- 1 Corinthians 12:11
- Ephesians 4:7
- Revelation 2:17

PONDER & PRAY

In a world that points us toward individuality and praises those who manage to set themselves apart from the crowd, we are called to consider our common ground. We are a part of the beloved, the brethren, the body of Christ. This week, ponder over those things that are true for all believers. What makes us the same? What unites us? Ask the Lord to show you ways in which you can take up your part in the whole. How can you pursue all the ways we can be there for one another?

TRINKET TO TREASURE

As we look at the balance between unity and diversity in the body of believers, our trinket is the snowflake. Scientists tell us that no two have ever or will ever be exactly alike. God used the same delightful variation when He made us! No two are just the same. Each of us is uniquely fashioned. And yet we fill a part in something bigger—the body, the Church. We may be as unique and diverse as the snowflakes, but packed together we make a divinely designed snowman!

CHAPTER 11

BALANCING OUR WISHES AND GOD'S WILL

"HE WHO DOES THE WILL OF GOD ABIDES FOREVER."

1 John 2:17 NKJV

I grew up in an area of the country where weather-watching is an all-consuming pastime. The weather was the first thing we tuned into the radio to check in the morning, and the last thing we stayed up to see on the local news before turning in for the night. If you ran into a friend or neighbor during the day, you'd most likely start your chat with comparing the levels in your rain gauges from last night's storm. Falling barometers, low-pressure systems, and Alberta clippers were discussed with ease over dinner. County maps were mastered early, from constant scrutiny of Doppler radar loops. Yardsticks were mounted to fence posts to calculate the depths of drifting snow. The equation for

CLEARING
✦ THE ✦
COBWEBS

When it comes to receiving gifts, would you rather do all your own choosing or be surprised?

calculating wind chill factors was stuck with a magnet on the fridge door. But for all our preoccupation with the weather, nary a one of us could bend it to our will. Sure, we might hope for a sunny, mild day for the church picnic. And we might pray for a few inches of fresh powder before the youth ski trip. But all the wishing and wanting in the world would not change the weather.

Now when it comes to the balance between our wishes and God's will, we're in much the same situation. Often, we'd like to bend God's plans to suit our wishes, just as we'd like to demand rain in the midst of a summer drought. But that'd be going at things backwards. The will of God won't waver under our efforts to influence it. His will stands. But God can mold our hearts so that our wishes begin to match His will and our desires fall in line with His!

1. Why did God choose David to be a king, according to Acts 13:22?

2. What is the promise of Psalm 37:4?

3. All of us eventually face a time when our first choice doesn't fall in line with God's will, and we know it. What did Jesus do in such a situation, according to Luke 22:42?

4. Jesus was not the only one willing to submit His will to God.

• What did John the Baptist declare in John 3:30?

• What did Paul declare in Galatians 2:20?

5. We live to do God's will.

Romans 12:2 — "And do not be _____ to this _____, but be _____ by the renewing of your _____, that you may _____ what is that _____ and _____ and _____ _____ of God" (NKJV).

6. What does Peter tell us to live for in 1 Peter 4:2?

*R*emember God's offer to Solomon, when he became king over Israel after David? God came to Solomon in a dream and offered to bless him. "What do you want, young Solomon? Shall I make you richer than any man on earth? Shall I destroy all your enemies and give you supremacy in the political world? Or would you rather have the promise of a long life? You may choose!" What an opportunity for Solomon! What man wouldn't want any of those three guarantees just as he's setting up his rule? It's almost like the genie and his three wishes! He could pick one and know it would be his. But Solomon deferred. He asked for the wisdom to lead God's people as

God would have him do so. He wanted the wisdom to do God's will! And because of Solomon's willingness to let go of his own desires for the sake of God's, the Lord was enormously pleased. In fact, God turned around and gave Solomon the wisdom he longed for, then threw in the wealth, longevity, and world domination he'd been willing to pass up!

Giving up our own wishes to do God's will can be a scary prospect. We're often afraid that God will ask us to do something hard. We don't like to let go and let God assume the leadership in case we don't like where He'll lead. But God's not trying to ensnare us or make our lives miserable. He wasn't asking Solomon a trick question, but He was pleased when Solomon chose to seek His will. God wants to grow us up, to bless us, and to bring glory to His own name. We needn't fear any of those things.

7. Interestingly enough, there are several verses in the Bible that actually say, "This is the will of God for you!" Here are a handful of them. What do each of these say is God's will for believers?

1 Thessalonians 4:3 —

1 Thessalonians 5:18 —

1 Peter 2:15 —

1 Peter 3:17 —

8. What is John's promise to those who do the will of God?

DIGGING DEEPER

Think your way through Bible stories. What men and women can you think of who were willing to let go of their own wishes, dreams, and plans for their lives to do instead what God asked them to do? Some had to make small adjustments, but others had their whole life turned upside down. What do their life stories teach us about God's will?

PONDER & PRAY

This week, pray that God would give you the desires of your heart. Ask that His ways would become dear to you, that His plans would excite your interest, that His words would echo in your heart and mind as you make decisions every day. Look back in your life, and see if you can discern God's hand and God's will guiding you along. Did things happen just as you thought they would? Do you still want the same things you wanted then? How has God been working in your heart?

TRINKET TO TREASURE

All the wishing in the world can't change the weather, and all our little wishes can't derail God's will. Our reminder of these truths is our trinket for this week — a rain gauge. We can't stand in God's way any more than we can stop the rain from falling, but we can learn to carry an umbrella and sing as we skip through the puddles! God gives us the desires of our hearts, if only we will let Him.

✦ NOTES & PRAYER REQUESTS ✦

CHAPTER 12

BALANCING WORKING AND WAITING

"MY SOUL WAITS FOR THE LORD MORE THAN THOSE WHO WATCH FOR THE MORNING—YES, MORE THAN THOSE WHO WATCH FOR THE MORNING."

Psalm 130:6 NKJV

I remember the day when, as a young freshman, my hour of waiting for the cafeteria to open for dinner was forever transformed. After an afternoon in the library stacks, I had decided to head back to the dormitories for a little while before suppertime. My route led me past the mailboxes, through the tunnel, and up into the fine arts hall, past the open doors of the choir room. Choir was in full swing, and my steps slowed to a halt at the piercingly beautiful sounds that filled the passage. I had never heard the like, but my very soul was captivated. The words were Latin, and the harmonies would have been at home in

CLEARING ✦ THE ✦ COBWEBS

If you know you're in for a long wait—airports, waiting rooms, jury duty—what do you take along to occupy yourself?

any cathedral. Transfixed, I made my way to a bench and stayed put fo the remainder of the rehearsal. I was hooked. The next day, I planned m schedule to include the musical interlude. By the end of the week, I wa a fixture—ready and waiting for choir to start, happily ensconced on cushioned bench in the sun. I waited for dinner every afternoon in tha spot, but I didn't like to "waste" my time luxuriating in the choir's ever changing repertoire. So I began packing handwork in my duffle bag While my mind was engaged in the beautiful harmonies ringing from th choir room, my hands were busy with cross-stitch. All those hours were balance between busy work and blissful waiting. I still have the piece completed that first year, a beautifully frame Christmas scene.

> *We have not even begun to see what God has in store for us. Even the best moments that He showers on us are hardly the appetizer for the banquet He has prepared. Hold on to your hats, girls, we've only just begun to experience all the delights God has prepared for us.*
>
> Sheila Walsh

We believers are waiting for something, too And we do not fritter away our hours of wait ing. Instead, we are encouraged to balance ou expectation with usefulness. It is one of the hall marks of the Christian life—working and wait ing. Our hands are busy even as we keep watch

1. Just what is it we're waiting for?

2. Christ's coming has been foretold, and is often described in the New Testament. Match up these verses, which vividly speak of Jesus' return.

___ Mark 13:26   a. The coming of the Lord is at hand.

___ Mark 13:36   b. "I am going away and coming back to you."

___ Luke 21:27   c. He shall come suddenly.

___ John 14:28   d. "I am coming as a thief."

___ Hebrews 10:37   e. He is coming with clouds, every eye will see Him.

___ James 5:8   f. The Son of Man will come in the clouds with glory.

___ Revelation 1:7   g. "Behold, I am coming quickly."

___ Revelation 3:11   h. He is coming with power and great glory.

___ Revelation 16:15   i. Yet a little while, and He who is coming will come.

3. How does 1 Corinthians 1:7 say we should wait for the day when Jesus returns?

4. Expectant. That's what we're to be. We're to live with an eagerness that expects something to happen any minute. "Now we live with a wonderful expectation because Jesus Christ rose again from the dead" (1 Pet. 1:3 NLT). And we're not the only ones waiting!

"For the _____ _____ of the _____ eagerly _____ for the _____ of the sons of God. For the _____ was subjected to futility, not willingly, but because of Him who subjected it in _____; because the _____ itself also will be _____ from the _____ of _____ into the glorious _____ of the children of God. For we know that the whole _____ _____ and _____ with _____ _____ together until now" —Romans 8:19–22 NKJV

e wait with bated breath, on pins and needles, at the edge of our seats. We wait in lines at the grocery store. We wait on delayed flights at the airport. We sit in waiting rooms at the hospital. Sometimes the waiting seems interminable—waiting for test results, for a verdict, for a check, for a buyer. Sometimes we wait with the impatience of youth—waiting to be old enough for makeup, for high-heeled shoes, for pierced ears. Sometimes we wait with restless excitement—waiting for birthdays, for picnics, for trips to Grandma's house, for Christmas morning, for summer vacation, and for the skies to be dark enough for the fireworks to begin on Independence Day. Waiting is a part of life.

5. Waiting and watching. The heart of the believer is always looking forward to the final fulfillment of all God's promises. After all, Jesus told us to watch!

• Why does Matthew 25:13 tell us to watch?

• When does Mark 13:35 say the return could be?

6. We can't just sit on a stump, contemplating cloud formations until the trumpet sounds. In fact, Paul is critical of those who won't make themselves useful in the body of believers. What does Paul have to say about those who neglect their work in 2 Thessalonians 3:11?

7. Instead, how are we to conduct ourselves, according to these verses?

- 1 Corinthians 4:12

- Ephesians 4:16

8. There are good things ahead, and we await them with eagerness. Paul said, "Meanwhile, the joyful anticipation deepens" (Rom. 8:21 MSG). It's in the *meanwhile* that we are now living, and it is in the *meanwhile* that we must find the balance between waiting and working. What does 2 Peter 3:14 say about living in the meanwhile?

DIGGING DEEPER

The idea of continuing to do what we know we should be doing is prevalent in Paul's writing. Consider this passage from 2 Timothy. What does Paul urge Timothy to do? Where does he say Timothy can find assurance that he's doing the right thing? And what does Scripture equip us for?

"But you must continue in the things which you have learned and been assured of, knowing from whom you have learned them, and that from childhood you have known the Holy Scriptures, which are able to make you wise for salvation through faith which is in Christ Jesus. All Scripture is given by inspiration of God, and is profitable for doctrine, for reproof, for correction, for instruction in righteousness, that the man of God may be complete, thoroughly equipped for every good work." —2 Timothy 3:14–17 NKJV

PONDER & PRAY

There is a saying which criticizes those who are "too heavenly minded to be any earthly good." This week, your prayer can be twofold. It's alright to live attuned to heaven's promise. We can await the Lord's return with eagerness and anticipation. Pray for a refreshing of that expectancy in your heart. But meanwhile, ponder ways in which you can work while you're waiting. What might the Lord have you busy about in the meantime?

TRINKET TO TREASURE

The promise of heaven's glories and our eagerness to see our Lord face to face can fill our hearts with expectation. But even in this anticipation, we must remember that we need balance. Our trinket this week is a reminder to balance our waiting with useful work—a needle and thread. We are to keep our hands busy about the Lord's work even as we keep an ear tuned to the Lord's coming.

✦ NOTES & PRAYER REQUESTS ✦

SHALL WE REVIEW?

1. Juggling balls.

When it comes to balancing everything in our lives, we may feel like we're in a juggling act. Some people make the juggling look so effortless, and often we feel like we've dropped the ball. But when we strive for a balance between our physical and spiritual needs, the Lord helps us find our rhythm.

2. A dog's collar.

Balancing our time and responsibilities is no easy feat! This trinket reminded us that every new responsibility we take on demands a commitment of our time and energy. Finding the proper balance means making tough choices, and sometimes saying no.

3. A pocket watch.

Life is filled with the unexpected, and finding the balance between our schedules and those pesky interruptions can be a challenge. This trinket reminds us that while punctuality and efficiency may be admirable, God's plans may differ from ours. We must face each interruption with the attitude that God is at work.

4. An ant.

To keep our sanity, our lives must have a balance of work and rest. We must work, but not obsessively. We must rest, but not become lazy. This week's trinket served to remind us to follow Solomon's advice to "consider the ant," who works with steady diligence in the summer months, and finds rest through the long winter.

5. A blindfold.

We used this trinket to remind us that we "walk by faith and not by sight" (2 Cor. 5:7 NKJV). The Christian walk is hardly a game of blind man's bluff, but we acknowledge and depend on things which are invisible to our eyes.

6. A string around your finger.

This is the week we talked about the balance between love and obedience in our lives. Love doesn't mean manipulating others—wrapping them around our fingers by saying, "If you *really* loved me you would . . . ." But there is truth in the statement that love is demonstrated through our actions. Jesus said, "If you love Me, keep My commandments" (John 14:15 NKJV).

7. A map.

Here we find a balance between faith and works. Just as a road map only does us any good if we believe in its accuracy and follow its directions, our faith only does anyone any good if we do something with it. What we say we believe must match up with what we do.

8. Paint swatches.

Paint swatches help us to find the perfect match, though in the process we pass over many things that could have made do just as well. This trinket was to serve as a reminder of the balance we must find between our wants and our needs. God knows just what we need, and He's provided the perfect match.

9. A bird in the hand.

We don't need to look beyond what God has given us, always striving for the next big thing. The old saying goes, "A bird in the hand is worth two in the bush." Balancing longing and contentment comes when we learn to be thankful for what God has given us, and when we learn that complete satisfaction won't really be ours until we're in glory.

10. A snowflake.

As we look at the balance between unity and diversity in the body of believers, our trinket is the snowflake. No two have ever or will ever be exactly alike. In the same way, each of us is uniquely fashioned. And yet we fill a part in something bigger—the body, the Church.

11. A rain gauge.

In our lives, we must learn the proper balance between our own will and God's will. Just as all the wishing in the world can't change the weather, all our little wishes can't derail God's will. We can't stand in God's way any more than we can stop the rain from falling, but we can learn to carry an umbrella and sing as we skip through the puddles! God gives us the desires of our hearts, if only we will let Him.

12. A needle and thread.

The promise of heaven's glories and our eagerness to see our Lord face to face can fill our hearts with expectation. But even in this anticipation, we must remember that we need balance. We balance our waiting with useful work—the good works God has planned for us.

WHAT SHALL WE STUDY NEXT?

Women of Faith® has a series of study guides on various topics to help you draw closer to God.

RECEIVING GOD'S LOVE

Have you ever meandered through the index of your hymnal and considered just how many hymns extol God's great love for us? "What Wondrous Love Is This?" "O the Deep, Deep Love of Jesus." "Jesus Loves Even Me." Consider for a moment what each of these song titles is saying, the message each conveys: "Love Divine, All Loves Excelling"—God's love for us exceeds any other love we might experience. "Jesus, Lover of My Soul"— We have a Savior who loves us for who we are on the inside. "O Perfect Love"—flawless, faultless, fervent, forever love. And look at some of the lines. "Amazing love, how can it be?" "I will sing of my Redeemer, and His wondrous love for me." "O, how He loves you and me." "Thy loving kindness is better than life." We sing them with familiarity, but do we consider the truth behind these lyrics?

God's love for us really is wondrous, perfect, deep, divine. In this study, we'll take the time to look at the key passages in our Bibles that talk about that love. We need to understand the precious nature of the love God holds out to us in order to receive it with our whole heart.

KNOWING GOD'S WORD

For many people, the thought of studying brings back unpleasant memories of school. Those were the days when we were told what we needed to know. We endured lectures, library-time, projects, and pop quizzes. Homework was the scourge of our young lives—dull, daily, and always due. We only learned what we needed to know for the test. We retained our knowledge just long enough to secure a passing grade, then promptly forgot it all. None of us really expected to need to know algebra outside of high school. And when we finally scraped our way through our senior year and across the graduation platform, we were determined never to open another textbook again.

Of course that's not everyone's experience. But still, most people retain the notion that learning takes place in the classroom, and when you're through with school, you're through with "book learning." And of course, that's not really the case. We can and do learn, and we needn't enroll in a class to do it. With a basic understanding of the tools we need and a willingness to apply ourselves to our studies, we can enjoy a lifetime of learning.

This Bible study has a two-fold purpose. First, it is designed to teach you how to study the Scriptures. It introduces you to the tools and techniques you need to know. And secondly, while we're learning how to study the Bible, we'll be learning what the Bible tells us about itself. This will give us a hands-on approach. We'll be learning something while we learn how to learn! Interested? I think this is going to be fun. Let's go!

GIVING GOD YOUR ALL

Are you familiar with the story, *The Emperor's New Clothes*? Two cunning con artists are able to take in an entire nation because nobody wants to look foolish. You see, they set themselves up as master tailors, and offer to create a new suit of clothes for the emperor. The emperor, being a trifle vain, is enormously pleased at the prospect of new finery . . . until the first fitting. With a knowing gleam in their eyes, the conniving tailors display their handiwork, made from a most remarkable fabric. This cloth is so fine, so rare, so miraculously wrought that only the best of men can see it. Those who are unable to see it are fools, unworthy of the position they hold. The emperor is stunned! He'd never considered himself a fool, but for the life of him he cannot see a thing in the tailor's hands. And so he pretends he can see what the others claim to hold. So do all his friends and associates, for no one wants to seem a fool. The suit of clothes is completed, and though they're a bit drafty to the emperor's way of thinking, he agrees to parade through the land, showing them off. But in the end, the truth comes out. There was no cloth. There were no clothes. Everyone has been pretending to see what was not there to begin with, rather than stand out as the only one who could not see.

Have you ever had a secret suspicion that you're missing out on something important in your Christian walk? This believer or that believer will talk about their walk of faith with words like *vibrant*, *intimate*, and *personal*. Their glowing description of their relationship with the divine makes you wonder if you're doing something wrong. Oh, you have faith. You do love God. But to call your dealings with the Lord *vibrant* would be going a little too far. You're not sure what you expected, but you know it wasn't this. But who wants to look foolish? If everyone else says their Christian life is so intimate and personal, ours had better be, too. So we all use the same words. We all nod with understanding when a friend shares about God's working in their hearts. But we wonder why God seems more an acquaintance than a friend to us.

Nobody wants to be labeled a "nominal" Christian. But what changes a life of nodding acquaintance to one of personal intimacy? In a word—surrender. Once we're willing to let God be God, to look to Him in every situation, to value His opinions over any others, to trust Him in every circumstance, and to do what He would have us to do—then the relationship we long for deepens, strengthens, and positively vibrates with vibrancy!

Do you trust God enough to let Him take the reigns? This study takes a look at what the Bible says about yielding to God, giving Him your all, and being able to say, "Not my will, but Thine be done."

LEADER'S GUIDE

Chapter 1

1. "Therefore I say to you, do not worry about your life, what you will eat; nor about the body, what you will put on. Life is more than food, and the body is more than clothing" (Luke 12:22, 23 NKJV). Sure, we have to take care of life's practical needs. But Jesus says not to worry so much over them. Life is far more than the lasagna we put on the table and the tennis shoes we put on our feet!

2. "For bodily exercise profits a little, but godliness is profitable for all things, having promise of the life that now is and of that which is to come" (1 Tim. 4:8 NKJV). Exercise is good for us, and most of us know we could use a little more of it. But Paul reminds believers that while taking care of our physical bodies is a good thing, we mustn't neglect our spiritual lives.

3. f, c, g, a, e, h, d, b

4. "Now the ones that fell among thorns are those who, when they have heard, go out and are choked with cares, riches, and pleasures of life, and bring no fruit to maturity" (Luke 8:14 NKJV). This describes those who hear God's Word, accept it as truth, and have every intention of doing what it says. But their lives are so full of other things, that the Word has no room to do its good work. Such individuals have too many cares, busy schedules, other goals to pursue, and more exciting things to do with their free time. They may have successful lives in the eyes of the world, but in God's eyes, their lives are disappointing, for they bear no fruit for His kingdom!

5. "Every **branch** in Me that does not **bear fruit** He takes away; and every **branch** that **bears fruit** He **prunes**, that it may bear **more fruit**" (NKJV). "You did not **choose** Me, but I **chose** you and **appointed** you that you should **go** and **bear fruit**, and that your **fruit** should **remain**" (NKJV).

6. "Abide in Me and I in you. As the branch cannot bear fruit of itself, unless it abides in the vine, neither can you, unless you abide in Me" (John 15:4 NKJV). We must abide in the Lord—stay close to Him, depend upon Him, draw strength from Him. Our solo efforts will be fruitless, but when we allow the Lord to work in and through our lives, His work flourishes. "By this My Father is glorified, that you bear much fruit; so you will be My disciples" (John 15:8 NKJV). What other motivation could we need than this? When we bear fruit in our lives, God is glorified!

Chapter 2

1. "Surely every man is **vapor**" (Ps. 39:11 NKJV). "From the **greatest** to the **lowliest**—all are **nothing** in his sight. If you **weigh** them on the **scales**, they are **lighter** than a **puff** of **air**" (NLT). "You do not know what will **happen tomorrow**. For what is your **life**? It is even a **vapor** that appears for a **little time** and then **vanishes** away" (James 4:14 NKJV).

2. "We finish our years like a sigh" (Ps. 90:9 NKJV). We never seem to have enough time to do all the things we'd like to do in our lifetime. Just when we seem to be catching our breath, we find nearly all our days have been spent. I wonder if David's sigh merely betokens the brevity of life, or if the sigh holds some emotion with it. Sighs of regret, sighs of relief, sighs of contentment?

3. "Redeeming the time, because the days are evil" (Eph. 5:16 NKJV). "Walk in wisdom toward those who are outside, redeeming the time" (Col. 4:5 NKJV). Redeeming has the idea of purchasing. In fact, its root is in the Latin, "to buy." We often say, "Time is money." What do we spend our time on?

4. "For all the Athenians and the foreigners who were there spent their time in nothing else but either to tell or to hear some new thing" (Acts 17:21 NKJV). We each have our own weaknesses. Talking on the phone, paging through magazines, watching television, reading books, going shopping, playing games—they can all take us away from our responsibilities. Whether intentionally or unintentionally, they help distract us from and avoid what we know we should be doing.

5. True and False answers:

_F_ Life is ours to enjoy. There is plenty of time for "religion" later on, after we've had our fun (Mark 13:33).

_T_ Our time is always ready (John 7:6).

_T_ Times of refreshing come from the presence of the Lord (Acts 3:19).

_T_ It's high time we snapped out of it and took notice. The time for which we've been waiting is close than we thought (Rom. 13:11).

_F_ We've nothing to worry about and can live as we please, for God has a soft spot in His heart for those of us who mean well (1 Pet. 1:17).

_T_ We're called to humble ourselves, and that's all. But God, in His own time, may choose to exalt us (1 Pet. 5:6).

Chapter 3

1. "The LORD brings the counsel of the nations to nothing; He makes the plans of the peoples of no effect. The counsel of the LORD stands forever, The plans of His heart to all generations" (Ps. 33:10, 11 NKJV). On a grand scale, even a world-wide scale, God is working in the lives of people. He is the one directing. He is the one whose plans will come to pass. Our own schemings and schedules will come to nothing if they are contrary to the Lord's purposes.

2. "A man's heart plans his way, but the LORD directs his steps" (Prov. 16:9 NKJV). We may have it all figured out in our heads, but in the end, our steps are directed by God.

3. "For it is God who works in you both to will and to do for His good pleasure" (Phil. 2:13 NKJV). Instead of facing every interruption as a roadblock, stop to consider why God has placed it in your path for that day. What may frustrate you as an utter inconvenience at first glance may be just the thing God has for you to do for Him! Remember, we are here to do His will. We are here for His good pleasure. We would do well to consider His plans before our own!

4. "'For My thoughts are not your thoughts, Nor are your ways My ways, ' says the LORD. 'For as the heavens are higher than the earth, So are My ways higher than your ways, And My thoughts than your thoughts'" (Is. 55:8, 9 NKJV). Why can't we understand the unexpected elements in our days? Because we can't understand God. And why can't we understand God? Simply because He's God and we're not! God's hasn't told us everything about His plans, and so we are left to trust that He knows best.

5. "Oh, the depth of the riches both of the wisdom and knowledge of God! How unsearchable are His judgments and His ways past finding out!" (Rom. 11:33 NKJV) Our understanding of God's ways just brushes the surface of something Paul compares to depths of riches. Though we seek them, they are unsearchable. Though we try to understand them, we'll never fully find them out. That is why we must have such faith!

6. g, d, a, e, b, h, c, f

7. "O LORD, I know the way of man is not in himself; it is not in man who walks t direct his own steps" (Jer. 10:23 NKJV). We aren't able to direct our own steps

Jeremiah says it isn't in us to do so. "Direct my steps by Your word, And let no iniquity have dominion over me" (Ps. 119:133 NKJV). The psalmist wisely turns to God's Word for direction. In it we can discover the kind of life pleasing to our Lord. "In all your ways acknowledge Him, And He shall direct your paths" (Prov. 3:6 NKJV).

8. "Now may the Lord direct your hearts into the love of God and into the patience of Christ" (2 Thess. 3:5 NKJV). To deal with interruptions in our schedules with grace, we need the very two things that Paul prays we will have—love like God's and patience like Christ's!

Chapter 4

1. e, c, a, f, b, d

2. "For even when we were with you, we commanded you this: If anyone will not work, neither shall he eat" (2 Thess. 3:10 NKJV). It's the same simple principle instituted by John Smith in the American colonies—one that saved many lives during those first, fierce winters. Those who do not work will not eat!

3. "Six days you shall do your work, and on the seventh day you shall rest, that your ox and your donkey may rest, and the son of your female servant and the stranger may be refreshed" (Ex. 23:12 NKJV). "Work shall be done for six days, but the seventh is the Sabbath of rest, holy to the LORD. Whoever does any work on the Sabbath day, he shall surely be put to death" (Ex. 31:15 NKJV).

4. "Oh, that I had wings like a dove! I would fly away and be at rest" (Ps. 55:6 NKJV). At some time or another, most of us would have loved to run away from it all.

5. "Come aside by yourselves to a deserted place and rest a while" (Mark 6:31 NKJV). Jesus didn't run His disciples into the ground with the work of the ministry. He wisely interspersed their work with times of quiet and rest. "Come to Me, all you who labor and are heavy laden, and I will give you rest. Take My yoke upon you and learn from Me, for I am gentle and lowly in heart, and you will find rest for your souls" (Matt. 11:28, 29 NKJV). Jesus calls to all of those who know what weariness is, and promises them rest. His words are so gentle: come to me, learn from me, find rest with me.

6. Proverbs 27:23 — Be diligent to know the state of your flocks. 2 Timothy 2:15 — Be diligent to present yourself approved. Hebrews 4:11 — Be diligent to enter the rest God has prepared for us. 2 Peter 1:10 — Be diligent to make your call sure. 2 Peter 1:14 — Be diligent to be found by Him in peace, blameless.

7. "Keep your heart with all diligence, For out of it spring the issues of life" (Prov. 4:23 NKJV). We need to take care of our responsibilities, knowing the state of our own flocks, so to speak. This takes hard work. But we cannot be lazy in keeping our hearts. Diligence plays a part in our physical lives as well as our spiritual lives. Why does Solomon urge us to keep our hearts with all diligence? Because our heart is the part of us that is us, and all our thoughts, decisions, choices, and actions have their beginnings within it.

Chapter 5

1. "Since the creation of the world His invisible attributes are clearly seen, being understood by the things that are made, even His eternal power and Godhead, so that they are without excuse" (Rom. 1:20 NKJV). Paul states that the created world reveals much to us about God, that no one has any excuse for missing the message.

2. "One generation shall praise your works to another, and shall declare Your mighty acts" (Ps. 145:4 NKJV). Everyone in the world has the wonders of creation to point them to the existence of God. But throughout Scripture and even today, there are men and women who are willing to tell other people about God. We can tell others how knowing God has changed our lives. We can give Him the glory in our successes and lean on Him with confidence during our struggles. God uses creation, but He uses Christians, too!

3. "For by Him all things were created that are in heaven and that are on earth, visible and invisible, whether thrones or dominions or principalities or powers. All things were created through Him and for Him" (Col. 1:16 NKJV). When we think of creation, we think of the sun and the moon, the land and the seas, the birds and the fishes, and Adam and Eve. What we often forget is that God also created things that we cannot readily observe. There is that which is seen, and that which is unseen. Visible and invisible.

4. "Where then is my hope? As for my hope, who can see it?" (Job 17:15 NKJV). It is said that while there is life, there is hope. Inseparable from our faith is the hope on which it depends. Hope is an intangible thing too, and yet it has great power to influence our lives.

5. "Now faith is the substance of things hoped for, the evidence of things not seen" (Heb. 11:1 NKJV). Faith is the substance of things hoped for. A life lived by faith is the evidence that all men can see—evidence of an invisible hope. If the spiritual world were like the wind, which we cannot see, then faith would be the kite. It depends on the wind to lift it up, and its flight stands as testimony to the wind's presence and power.

6. "For we walk by faith, not by sight" (2 Cor. 5:7 NKJV). We need not rely on the things we can see and touch in order to live. Faith requires us to depend on things we cannot see, to hope in things we will not see until they come to pass.

7. "But as for me, I trust in You, O LORD; I say, 'You are my God'" (Ps. 31:14 NKJV). "But it is good for me to draw near to God; I have put my trust in the Lord GOD, That I may declare all Your works" (Ps. 73:28 NKJV). It is good to draw near to God and to declare His working in your heart and life. Tell others what He has done for you, because your testimony may be just the thing needed to bring another seeking heart to God in faith.

Chapter 6

1. "God demonstrates His own love toward us, in that while we were still sinners, Christ died for us" (Rom. 5:8 NKJV). Even before we knew we needed Him, God sent Jesus to pay for our sins. He demonstrated His love by sacrificing Himself on our behalf.

2. "Therefore you shall love the LORD your God, and keep His charge, His statutes, His judgments, and His commandments always" (Deut. 11:1 NKJV). Moses commands them in the very same breath—love the Lord your God and keep His commandments. Look how thorough he is, too! He uses every synonym in the book for the book—charge, statutes, judgments, and commandments!

3. "Inasmuch as these people draw near with their mouths And honor Me with their lips, But have removed their hearts far from Me, And their fear toward Me is taught by the commandment of men" (Is. 29:13 NKJV). These people are only giving lipservice to God. They say all the right things, but their heart isn't in any of it. *The Message* translates this same verse nicely: "These people make a big show of saying the right thing, but their hearts aren't in it. Because they act like they're worshiping me but don't mean it."

4. "He who does not **love** Me does not **keep** My **words**" (John 14:24 NKJV). "If you **keep** My commandments, you will **abide** in My **love**, just as I have **kept** My Father's commandments and **abide** in His **love**" (John 15:10 NKJV).

5. "Therefore know that the LORD your God, He is God, the faithful God who keeps covenant and mercy for a thousand generations with those who love Him and keep His commandments" (Deut. 7:9 NKJV). "I pray, LORD God of heaven, O great and awesome God, You who keep Your covenant and mercy with those who love You and observe Your commandments" (Neh. 1:5 NKJV). Nehemiah quotes God's promise almost word for word in His prayer.

6. "For this is the love of God, that we keep His commandments. And His commandments are not burdensome" (1 John 5:3 NKJV). Love means obedience. Yes, we must obey God. But He doesn't ask too much of us. Our salvation frees us from the slavery of sin. But not to tie us down with a greater burden. These words seem a familiar echo of Jesus' own invitation to the weary to come to Him, "My yoke easy and My burden is light" (Matt. 11:30 NKJV)

7. "If anyone loves Me, he will keep My word; and My Father will love him, and We will come to him and make Our home with him" (John 14:23 NKJV). Those who love God and keep His word will find a wonderful promise fulfilled—God Himself will make His home in them.

Chapter 7

1. "Knowing that a man is not justified by the works of the law but by faith in Jesus Christ, even we have believed in Christ Jesus, that we might be justified by faith in Christ and not by the works of the law; for by the works of the law no flesh shall be justified" (Gal. 2:16 NKJV). Paul is adamant that we are justified by faith in Jesus. "You see then that a man is justified by works, and not by faith only" (James 2:24 NKJV). And here we have James saying faith isn't enough, but that our works justify us. Huh?

2. "They profess to know God, but in works they deny Him, being abominable, disobedient, and disqualified for every good work" (Titus 1:16 NKJV). Faith is what saves us, but no one can see our faith. What they can see is the evidence of our faith—our behavior, our deeds, our works! We may not be able to see what's in the heart of others, but by their works they either glorify God or deny Him.

3. "What does it **profit**, my brethren, if someone **says** he has **faith** but does not have **works**? Can **faith save** him?" (James 2:14 NKJV). "Thus also faith **by itself**, if it does not have **works**, is **dead**" (James 2:17 NKJV). "But someone will say, 'You have **faith**

and I have **works.**' **Show me** your faith **without** your works, and I will **show you** my faith **by** my works" (James 2:18 NKJV).

4. "But do you want to know, O foolish man, that faith without works is dead?" (James 2:20 NKJV). A faith that is claimed, but has no effect on our lives is as good as dead. "For as the body without the spirit is dead, so faith without works is dead also" (James 2:26 NKJV). A lifeless faith shows no sign of its existence.

5. "Do you see that faith was working together with his works, and by works faith was made perfect?" (James 2:22 NKJV). They go hand in hand, working together. Faith is made perfect by the works that flow out of it. We could also say that our works make our faith complete. The works, in and of themselves, don't save us. But they do demonstrate that our faith is real, vibrant, and growing.

6. "For we are His workmanship, created in Christ Jesus for good works, which God prepared beforehand that we should walk in them" (Eph. 2:10 NKJV). Good works were in the original blueprints!

7. c, e, b, a, d

8. "Who is wise and understanding among you? Let him show by good conduct that his works are done in the meekness of wisdom" (James 3:13 NKJV). If we are wise, we do good works with an attitude of meekness. "And let our people also learn to maintain good works, to meet urgent needs, that they may not be unfruitful" (Titus 3:14 NKJV). We need to learn not just how to do good works, but how to maintain them our whole life long. We need to establish a pattern of living. "And let us consider one another in order to stir up love and good works" (Heb. 10:24 NKJV). Good works don't just happen. We need to be thinking about one another, looking for needs. And we need to stir up those good works intentionally.

9. "Let your light so shine before men, that they may see your good works and glorify your Father in heaven" (Matt. 5:16 NKJV). "Having your conduct honorable among the Gentiles, that when they speak against you as evildoers, they may, by your good works which they observe, glorify God in the day of visitation" (1 Pet. 2:12 NKJV). Good works are just that—good. But more than that, they testify to all who see us. They point to God and bring Him glory.

Chapter 8

1. "And Abraham called the name of the place, **The-LORD-Will-Provide**; as it is said to this day, 'In the Mount of the LORD it shall be **provided**'" (Gen. 22:14 NKJV). "You **visit** the earth and **water** it, You greatly **enrich** it; The river of God is full of water; You **provide** their grain, For so You have **prepared** it" (Ps. 65:9 NKJV).

2. "Don't be like them, because your Father knows exactly what you need even before you ask him!" (Matt. 6:8 NLT). Before we know it for ourselves, He's aware of our every want and need.

3. "And God will generously provide all you need. Then you will always have everything you need and plenty left over to share with others" (2 Cor. 9:8 NLT). God is abundant in His provision for us. The promise is that we'll always have everything we need. Not only that, we'll have enough left over that we can share with others.

4. "And don't worry about food—what to eat and drink. Don't worry whether God will provide it for you" (Luke 12:29 NLT). God's provision frees us from worry.

5. "You can be sure that no immoral, impure, or greedy person will inherit the Kingdom of Christ and of God. For a greedy person is really an idolater who worships the things of this world" (Eph. 5:5 NLT). Greed is idolatry. Ouch!

6. d, a, e, f, b, c

7. "By doing this they will be storing up their treasure as a good foundation for the future so that they may take hold of real life" (1 Tim. 6:19 NLT). Paul compares storing up treasure with taking hold of real life. Eternal life with Jesus—what greater treasure could we have? "Then the Almighty himself will be your treasure. He will be your precious silver" (Job 22:25 NLT). God Himself will be our treasure. How great is that?

Chapter 9

1. "'Vanity of vanities,' says the Preacher; 'Vanity of vanities, all is vanity'" (Eccl. 1:2 NKJV). In other words, "Everything is meaningless" (NLT). Solomon describes his attempts to find meaning and satisfaction in all the things the world has to offer—building things, growing things, accumulating things, enjoying things, knowing things—but finds that none give the lasting contentment for which his soul longs.

2. "The **eye** is not **satisfied** with **seeing**, Nor the **ear filled** with **hearing**" (Eccl. 1:8 NKJV)."The **leech** has two **daughters**—Give and **Give**! There are three things that are never **satisfied**, Four never say, '**Enough!**': The **grave**, The **barren womb**, The **earth** that is not satisfied with **water**—And the **fire** never says, '**Enough!**'" (Prov. 30:15, 16 NKJV). "He who **loves silver** will not be **satisfied** with **silver**; Nor he who **loves abundance**, with **increase**. This also is **vanity**" (Eccl. 5:10 NKJV).

3. "My soul longs, yes, even faints For the courts of the LORD; My heart and my flesh cry out for the living God" (Ps. 84:2 NKJV). The soul longs to be with God. David even says his flesh cries out for it. "My soul breaks with longing For Your judgments at all times" (Ps. 119:20 NKJV). The psalmist says that he longs so intensely for God's Word that his soul seems to break.

4. "For He satisfies the longing soul, And fills the hungry soul with goodness" (Ps. 107:9 NKJV). The needs of our hearts can only be satisfied by God. True enough, we may try other means. Often we don't even realize the restlessness we feel is in our very souls!

5. "Not that I speak in regard to need, for I have learned in whatever state I am, to be content" (Phil. 4:11 NKJV). Paul knew times of peace and plenty. But he also endured shipwrecks, mob riots, death threats, and prison time. But Paul had learned not to base his level of contentment on outward circumstances.

6. "Now godliness with contentment is great gain" (1 Tim. 6:6 NKJV). Have you ever secretly envied the excitement and luxury enjoyed by those with heaps of money? Godliness is a good thing. But Paul goes a step further in declaring that when we live godly and are content with it, *that* is great!

7. "Let your conduct be without covetousness; be content with such things as you have. For He Himself has said, 'I will never leave you nor forsake you'" (Heb. 13:5 NKJV). The writer of Hebrews seems to shame us into contentment. After all, how could we long for anything more when we have God Himself with us?

8. "For I know that my Redeemer lives, And He shall stand at last on the earth; And after my skin is destroyed, this I know, That in my flesh I shall see God, Whom I shall see for myself, And my eyes shall behold, and not another. How my heart yearns within me!" (Job 19:25–27 NKJV). Job knows that he will see God for himself someday, and his heart yearns for that time. "For now we see in a mirror, dimly, but then face to face. Now I know in part, but then I shall know just as I also am known" (1 Cor. 13:12 NKJV). Paul assures us that though our understanding now is dim and imperfect, we will one day see things face to face. Then we will know just as we are known.

Chapter 10

1. "Your hands have made me and fashioned me, An intricate unity" (Job 10:8 NKJV). What a beautiful description of ourselves—an intricate unity!

2. "So we, being many, are one body in Christ, and individually members of one another" (Rom. 12:5 NKJV). Paul compares all the members of the community of faith, the Church, to a body—the body of Christ. Each of us has a part to play, and yet we all function together as a whole. Interrelated and interdependent.

3. "Now I plead with you, brethren, by the name of our Lord Jesus Christ, that you all speak the same thing, and that there be no divisions among you, but that you be perfectly joined together in the same mind and in the same judgment" (1 Cor. 1:10 NKJV). We can hardly work effectively together if we are busy arguing amongst ourselves. Paul says, "let there be no divisions." We like to think about the diversity to be found among all the members, but Paul would rather have us focus on the unity we need. "Be of the same mind together!"

4. "From whom the whole body, joined and knit together by what every joint supplies, according to the effective working by which every part does its share, causes growth of the body for the edifying of itself in love" (Eph. 4:16 NKJV). "That their hearts may be encouraged, being knit together in love" (Col. 2:2 NKJV). "Holding fast to the Head, from whom all the body, nourished and knit together by joints and ligaments, grows with the increase that is from God" (Col. 2:19 NKJV). We are knit together—woven together, interrelated, supporting one another, and stronger together than we could ever be alone.

5. "In this way we are like the various parts of a human body. Each part gets its meaning from the body as a whole, not the other way around. The body we're talking about is Christ's body of chosen people. Each of us finds our meaning and function as a part of his body. But as a chopped-off finger or cut-off toe we wouldn't amount to much, would we?" (Rom. 12:4, 5 MSG).

6. First Corinthians 12 is all about the body of Christ. Paul's message is clear. We're all part of something bigger. We need to work together. God has put us where He wants us. None of us can stand alone. We need to accept our place in the body, and fill our role with joy.

7. John 13:34 — Love one another. Romans 12:10 — Be kindly affectionate to one another. Romans 15:7 — Receive one another. 1 Corinthians 12:25 — Care for one another. Galatians 5:13 — Serve one another. Galatians 6:2 — Bear one another's burdens. Ephesians 4:32 — Be kind to one another and forgive one another. 1 Thessalonians 5:11 — Comfort and edify one another. Hebrews 3:13 — Exhort one another. James 5:16 — Confess your sins to one another and pray for one another. 1 Peter 3:8 — Have compassion for one another. 1 Peter 4:9 — Be hospitable to one another. 1 Peter 4:10 — Minister to one another with your God-given gifts. And these are just a sampling of the "one anothers" in the New Testament!

8. "Behold, how good and how pleasant it is For brethren to dwell together in unity!" (Ps. 133:1 NKJV). When we are working together as we should, our unity is a glimpse of heaven's perfection!

Chapter 11

1. "He raised up for them David as king, to whom also He gave testimony and said, 'I have found David the son of Jesse, a man after My own heart, who will do all My will'" (Acts 13:22 NKJV). We often hear about the first part of God's praise of David. Who wouldn't want to be known as a man or woman after God's own heart? But what about the next crucial phrase, "who will do all My will"? We cannot love God without obeying Him. And we cannot receive such high praise from God if we are unwilling to do His will.

2. "Delight yourself also in the LORD, And He shall give you the desires of your heart" (Ps. 37:4 NKJV). This is the very thing mentioned in the introduction to today's lesson. When David says God will give us the desires of our hearts, he's not saying God will give us whatever we want. He means that God will change our heart's desires. God will make us to desire what He wants us to desire.

3. "Father, if it is Your will, take this cup away from Me; nevertheless not My will, but Yours, be done" (Luke 22:42 NKJV). Jesus knew clearly which way His path was leading. He knew that pain and death would soon claim Him. And in His honest prayer to the Father, He asked if there was any other way. But no matter what, Jesus submitted to God's plans — "Not My will, but Yours, be done."

4. "He must increase, but I must decrease" (John 3:30 NKJV). We hear it a lot nowadays — "it's not about me!" This is the very attitude Jesus' forerunner and cousin adopted from the beginning. "I have been crucified with Christ; it is no longer I who live, but Christ lives in me; and the life which I now live in the flesh I live by faith in the Son of God, who loved me and gave Himself for me" (Gal. 2:20 NKJV). Paul lived to do the Lord's will, so much so that he described it as Christ living in him, working through him.

5. "And do not be **conformed** to this **world**, but be **transformed** by the renewing of your **mind**, that you may **prove** what is that **good** and **acceptable** and **perfect will** of God" (Rom. 12:2 NKJV).

6. "That he no longer should live the rest of his time in the flesh for the lusts of men, but for the will of God" (1 Pet. 4:2 NKJV). We don't live to satisfy our own whims and appetites. We live to do God's will.

7. "For this is the will of God, your sanctification" (1 Thess. 4:3 NKJV). "In everything give thanks; for this is the will of God in Christ Jesus for you" (1 Thess. 5:18 NKJV). "For this is the will of God, that by doing good you may put to silence the ignorance of foolish men" (1 Pet. 2:15 NKJV). "For it is better, if it is the will of God, to suffer for doing good than for doing evil" (1 Pet. 3:17 NKJV).

8. "And the world is passing away, and the lust of it; but he who does the will of God abides forever" (1 John 2:17 NKJV). When everything else falls apart in the end, we shall remain and abide forever with the Lord.

Chapter 12

1. "Be patient, brethren, until the coming of the Lord" (James 5:7 NKJV). We await our Lord's return.

2. f, c, h, b, i, a, e, g, d

3. "Eagerly waiting for the revelation of our Lord Jesus Christ" (1 Cor. 1:7 NKJV). Eagerly. With great eagerness and expectation. Like a child waiting for Christmas morning, or a mother-to-be during her ninth month of pregnancy. Those who are eager look forward with a single-minded intensity towards that for which they hope.

4. "For the **earnest expectation** of the **creation** eagerly **waits** for the **revealing** of the sons of God. For the **creation** was subjected to futility, not willingly, but because of Him who subjected it in **hope**; because the **creation** itself also will be **delivered** from the **bondage** of **corruption** into the glorious **liberty** of the children of God. For we know that the whole **creation groans** and **labors** with **birth pangs** together until now" (Rom. 8:19–22 NKJV).

5. "Watch therefore, for you know neither the day nor the hour in which the Son of Man is coming" (Matt. 25:13 NKJV). Nobody knows, so we must watch and be ready at any hour of the day. "Watch therefore, for you do not know when the master of the house is coming—in the evening, at midnight, at the crowing of the rooster, or in the morning" (Mark 13:35 NKJV). Any hour of the day or night may be the time God has chosen for Jesus' return.

6. "For we hear that there are some who walk among you in a disorderly manner, not working at all, but are busybodies" (2 Thess. 3:11 NKJV). Those who refuse to do their part are called disorderly and busybodies.

7. "We labor, working with our own hands" (1 Cor. 4:12 NKJV). Even Paul, the traveling preacher, wasn't afraid to sully his hands with honest work. Yes, God had appointed him to be an apostle, but he managed to work hard as a tentmaker as well. Paul was never a burden to his brothers and sisters in Christ. "The whole body, joined and knit together by what every joint supplies, according to the effective working by which every part does its share, causes growth of the body for the edifying of itself in love" (Eph. 4:16 NKJV). See that little phrase, "every part does its share"? Yes, we are waiting with great anticipation for the Lord's return. But in the meantime, we each have a part to play. God has works for us to do—the very good works for which we were created!

8. "And so, dear friends, while you are waiting for these things to happen, make every effort to live a pure and blameless life. And be at peace with God" (2 Pet. 3:14 NLT). We have work we can do with our hands. We have work that needs doing in our hearts. While we are waiting, we balance our time with useful work.

✦ NOTES ✦

✦ NOTES ✦

✦ NOTES ✦

The Complete Women of Faith®
Study Guide Series

Amazing Freedom

Overcoming Fear

Experiencing Spiritual Intimacy

Contagious Joy

Adventurous Prayer

Receiving God's Goodness

Giving God Your All

Living a Life of Balance

Managing Your Moods

Cultivating Contentment

Discovering God's Will for Your Life

Living in Jesus

Finding God in the Broken Places

Living Above Worry and Stress

Understanding Purpose

Knowing God's Word

Encouraging One Another

A Life of Worship

Receiving God's Love

Embracing God's Design for Your Life

WOMEN of FAITH™
STUDY GUIDE SERIES

To find these and other inspirational products visit your local Christian retailer.
www.thomasnelson.com